FOR MY MOTHER

Through your eyes I learned to understand
the true value of things—
nothing is junk that gives us joy.
You will always, always, always be
the joyful part of me.

First published in the United States of America in 2018 by
Rizzoli International Publications, Inc.
300 Park Avenue South, New York, NY 10010
www.rizzoliusa.com

Photographs: **Carter Berg**
Book design: **Aoife Wasser**
Editor: **Ellen Nidy**

2018 2019 2020 2021 2022 / 10 9 8 7 6 5 4 3 2 1

ISBN-13: 978-0-8478-6210-8

Library of Congress Control Number: 2018941591

Printed and bound in China

Distributed to the U.S. trade by Random House

THE JOY OF JUNK

MARY
RANDOLPH CARTER

THE JOY OF JUNK

MARY RANDOLPH CARTER

Photography by Carter Berg

Go right ahead, fall in love with the wackiest things, find the worth in the
worthless and, rescue and recycle the curious objects that give life and happiness
to the places we call home!

RIZZOLI
NEW YORK

New York · Paris · London · Milan

CONTENTS

8 THE JOY OF JUNKING

26 AN APARTMENT IS NOTHING BUT A BOX... Mary Randolph Carter

48 HOME IS WHERE YOUR HORSE IS Buffy Birrittella

68 BRIMFIELD MARKET

72 BRINGING THE OUTSIDE INSIDE Renée Parker Werner

90 PICKING & PRESERVING AMERICA'S STORIES Mike Wolfe

110 ANTIQUE ARCHAEOLOGY

112 LIFE IN THE SLOW LANE Shari Elf

130 SO HAPPY TOGETHER Bunny Williams and John Rosselli

144 COUNTRY LIVING FAIRS

148 MEN AT WORK John Ross and Don Carney

162 YOU ARE WHAT YOU LOVE Lisa Eisner

174 THE ROSE BOWL

178 MAKING ROOM FOR THE NEW Corinne Warner

192 RUST IN PEACE Bobby Furst

202 ANTIQUES AT THE BARN

206 A PASSION FOR FASHION Daniela Kamiliotis

216 CABINETS OF CURIOSITIES Clare Graham

230 TALES FROM A DOLL'S HOUSE Jane Ives

242 TREASURES FROM THE TRASH Nelson Molina

256 THE BEST THINGS IN LIFE ARE FREE Mary Stufano

262 THE JUNKERS' GUIDE

INTRODUCTION

THE JOY OF JUNKING

Let me state right from the beginning that I love junk, I love the hunt for junk, I love those heart-stopping moments when you see something before you on a cluttered table at a flea market or a yard sale and before you can even ask, "How much?" you're clutching it because you have to have it... and there's that lurking danger that the person standing over your shoulder or even right next to you might grab it! Then, there's the haggle, that junker/dealer sparring match that begins with, "How much?" What's your best price? Can you do better? (Oh, what fun!) My mouth is watering just to think that right now there is a flea market out there with treasures waiting to be found, haggled over, and won... and I'm not there!

So, why am I here writing this book, pouring my heart out to you instead of out on the prowl for precious bounty? Because after decades of junking I had to figure out why. Why do we do it? Why do we love it?

And so I decided to hit the junk trails all over America to seek out the sage veterans of flea markets, yard sales, boot sales, junk shops, auctions, estate sales, stoop sales, thrift shops, recycling centers, and even dumpsters who hunt for it, buy it, curate it, live with it, sell it, and most of all *CAN'T LIVE WITHOUT IT!*

Opposite: Jumping for joy at the Rose Bowl Flea Market in Pasadena, California. For more on this monthly junker's extravaganza, see page 174.

Snapshot memories along the junking trail captured by my partner-in-junk—my son Carter Berg, seen with his Rose Bowl find—a spiffy sock monkey wearing a bandanna just like his, middle row, far left. We traveled from coast-to-coast hunting down treasures at America's legendary flea markets from the Rose Bowl in California to Brimfield in Massachusetts, as well as vintage havens like Mike Wolfe's Antique Archaeology in Nashville (that's me beaming at the entrance, top row, far right). More to come on all the journeys, including tips on junker's garb, like my painted & patched overalls with a message, middle row, far right, and my never-leave-home-without-it junker's vest, top row, second from left. Check out my Junker's Guide on page 262 for some of the great junking spots around the U.S.A. It's always the right time to hunt for junk!

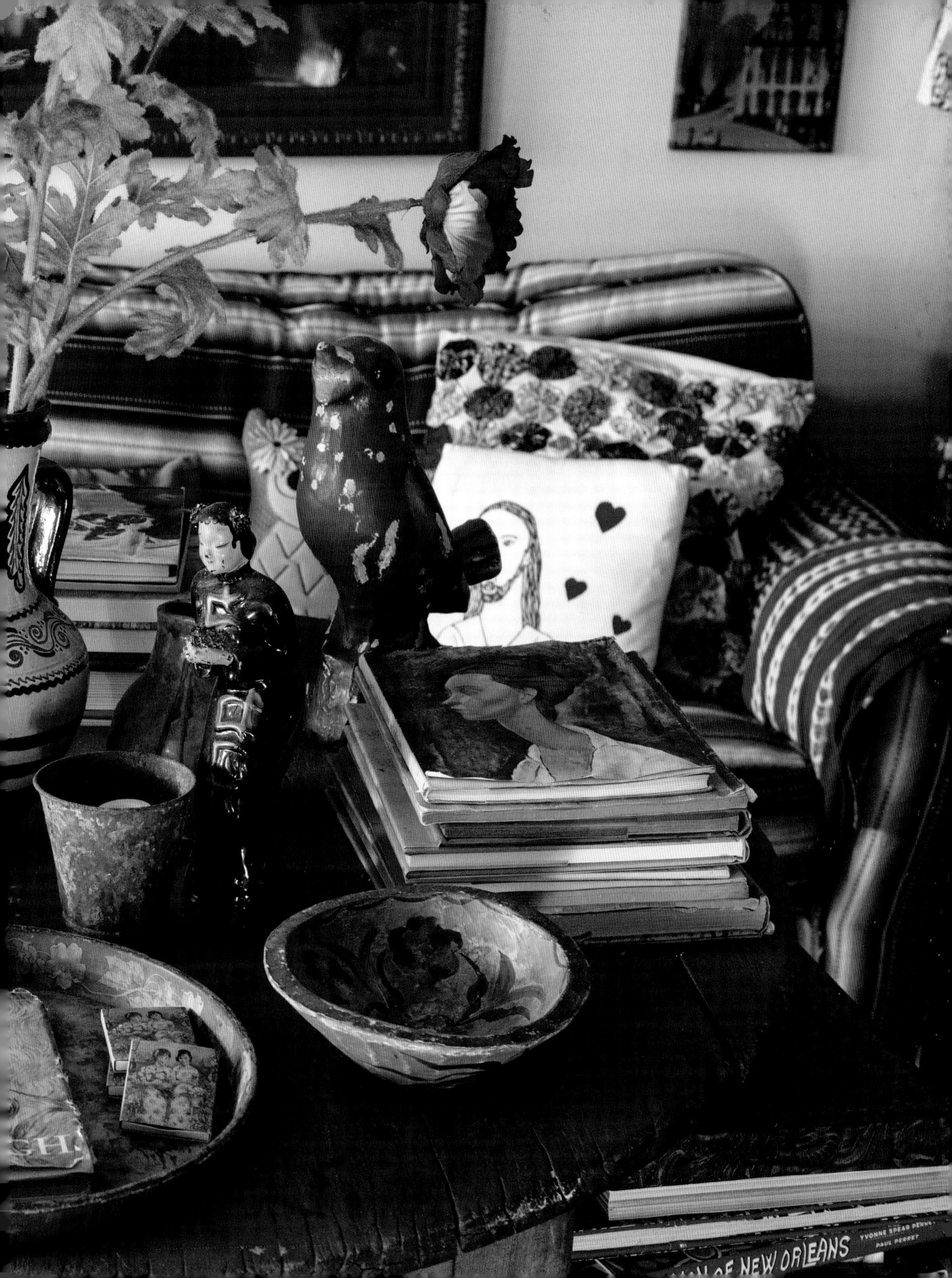
OF NEW ORLEANS
PAUL PERRET

BE PREPARED

I'm sitting at my desk preparing, as I always do, for the glorious day of junking ahead. It's a good idea to make a plan, a list of what you might be looking for on your hunt. That handwritten list will be the first thing I stick into my junker's vest as I set out and sometimes the last thing I take a look at. But my good intentions are to use the list as a junker's compass. Sometimes when you're out there in the fields of junk surrounded by so much incredible stuff—well, you know, it can very often go to your head, leave you spinning out of control, make you impulsive and greedy—"I must have this and this and this!" The list, then, can remind you of what you were really looking for. In the country I scour the local newspapers and online for tag sales, estate sales, and auctions. Map out the best route and the best timing to get there…first! Of course, even the best-laid plans or the most thought-out list can be flung to the winds when something or someplace strikes your fancy and you go totally off the grid. I say, "That's all right! Go right ahead!" Fall in love with the wackiest thing you'd never even thought of, but there it is and you are smitten! Oh, how delicious. No one can prepare for a junker's love at first sight!

*BEFORE YOU GO...

check out newspapers or go online to find tag sales or flea markets that are happening while you're there. This is a really good idea if you're traveling and are unfamiliar with the local junking turf.

*IT'S ALWAYS GOOD TO CONNECT WITH...

friends who live in the area and know markets and routes that are worth pursuing. Even better if they can go with you! Don't be a hero and go it alone.

*LAY OUT EVERYTHING THE NIGHT BEFORE...

—your junker's uniform, vest, cart, extra bags, camera, and charge your phone! Get a good night's sleep! Set your alarm for earlyish, and have that pot of coffee ready to perk!

Opposite: Making my list at my cluttered desk surrounded by favorite finds and gifts, like the red and white pointing-hand cupboard with my initials from my son Sam.

Previous Pages: Curating a tabletop: Because we often entertain large gatherings in our living room, the idea of having a table pulled up in front of the sofa (perfect height for plates of food!) was not that unorthodox.

COMFORTABLE CLOTHES ARE THE RULE

I love to wear a long-sleeved shirt layered over a T-shirt with baggy overalls or, on a really hot day, loose-fitting cotton pants.

THE JUNKER'S VEST:

An essential part of your uniform. Read all about it on the following pages.

ON THE HEAD:

A baseball hat or something to keep the sun off your face and to prevent the top of your head from burning. A small umbrella, like the child's variety, seen at left, can help a lot, and is easily stowed in a big straw bag like the one I'm carrying.

Tip: I really like a fishing cap with the extra-long bill or a baseball hat. Look for those with open-air mesh on the sides. So much cooler! That's not to say I haven't chosen to wear a funky felt hat or wide-brim straw. Whatever suits your junker's style!

ON THE FOOTSIES:

Though you might be inclined to wear flip-flops or sandals on a very hot day, consider the terrain and the weather before you decide. (As seen at left, mismatched espadrilles work!) If foul weather is in the forecast, I sometimes wear my rubber clogs. High boots can be really hot. A pair of thin socks is always a good idea. The last thing you want is to hobble around with blisters.

SUNGLASSES:

Though sunglasses tend to get in the way (I'm always taking them off to take a closer look at stuff), if you must, then attach them to a bright colored cord, Croakies or Chums.

Tip: REI.com has a cool assortment.

JUNK TIME:

Wear a big watch, preferably with an alarm on it, to remind you when you're meeting friends, it's time to drink some water, eat a snack, or it's fifteen minutes to flea market closing!

Tip: Check out the Internet for watches that talk to you as you're hunting. I found one on Amazon—the Ladies 4-Alarm Talking Watch that allows you to set four alarms and a nice woman (Siri's cousin?) speaks to you softly that it's time!

COME RAIN OR COME SHINE:

Take a handy fold-up rain poncho in your vest, and keep a pair of wellies, muck boots, or old sneakers in the trunk.

A COOLER IN THE CAR:

Filled with bottled water, juices, carrot sticks, fruit, almonds for a long day of junking, particularly if you're driving from tag sale to flea market. You won't want to waste time stopping for food. Eat a good breakfast in the morning.

JUNK DRIVERS:

If you do drive and junk be aware of normal drivers on the road, particularly those behind you. If you see something that appears to be a roadside pull-over possibility—no jamming on the brakes! Pull over slowly and take a look. I try to warn those poor unsuspecting drivers behind me with my "I Brake for Junk" bumper sticker. (Look for yours in the pages of the book and put it to work!!)

Opposite: All decked out head-to-toe for a hot day of junking at the Brimfield Antique Flea Market in July. Check out this year's dates in my Junker's Guide at the back of the book or go online to brimfieldantiquefleamarket.com

THE JUNKERS VEST

I've always considered "junking" a form of sport. Therefore, like any sport, fishing, for example, it goes without saying that dressing for the game is not only necessary, but gives you an advantage in a highly competitive field. Years ago I picked up my first fisherman's vest (at a flea market, of course) and realized it was the pièce de résistance for fishing at flea markets. Every pocket became a place to store all the essentials needed for the hunt. No longer was it necessary to encumber myself with a pocketbook and then waste precious time digging in it for the tool needed at the moment.

Tip: Vintage fishing vests are likely found in the racks of vintage clothes scattered throughout most markets. Or shop for vintage fishing vests online at sites like eBay, Amazon, and Etsy. (I just saw one on eBay for $19.95 with a gazillion pockets! I might beat you to it!)

THE LIST:

Jot down things you'll be on the prowl for. Include things like funny one-of-a-kind presents for birthdays, holidays, weddings, and the like. Think of the list as your junker's compass. Things can get a little overwhelming when you are out there hunting and glancing at your list can help you reset focus.

A JUNKER'S JOURNAL:

I used to haul my trusty old Polaroid camera and snap each find and tape it into a notebook. Today we can do that with the cameras on our phones, as well as archive all the pertinent info—date found, where, dealer's card, website, cost, receipt, etc. in the electronic notebook. Still, being old school, I guess, I have to always have a mini composition book and Sharpie close at hand! That night I still tape everything into a large composition book with notes on the dealer's wares.

A MAGNET:

For testing metals. If you're looking for gold or silver a magnet won't tell you if it's gold or silver, but it will tell you that it's not. If the magnet sticks to the item, then it is NOT gold or silver. If it doesn't stick there's a chance it is gold or silver, but more testing has to be done. *Tip:* If you're really into estate jewelry and want to identify the real from the fake, pick up a Neo (Neodymium) pocket magnet metal tester.

A SMALL MAGNIFYING GLASS:

To look for chips, cracks, dates, marks, names of artists, and manufacturing trademarks. *Tip:* My old Swiss Army Knife actually has a magnifying glass attached, as well as a lot of handy tools like scissors and a corkscrew to open that bottle of wine at the end of a big day!

WASH 'N DRI TOWELETTES:

Because those flea market treasures are often grimy, and because you'd be hard pressed to find a sink out there, take along some handy towelettes. While you're at it, bring along a portable pack of tissues—very handy when the Portosan has run out of TP.

SUNBLOCK AND SOME FORM OF ASPIRIN:

Essential, particularly when you're out in the heat. (Tips for Extreme Junking coming up!)

MONEY!

Today, the big difference in the flea market experience is that almost every vendor is set up with a credit card device. Having said that, it's always good to have some cash and checks available for more often than not the dealer who has the thing that you want the most doesn't take plastic! Just bring proper identification.

Opposite: One of my many junker's vests decorated with vintage patches, pins, and peace signs. Each pocket holds an essential tool to support a successful junker's hunt.

JUNKER'S M.O.:

When I hit an establishment or flea market, no matter how large or small, my modus operandi is the same. Case the place before making a purchase. (This is admittedly hard, if not virtually impossible, at a really huge market, but still I try.)

JUNKER'S CAVEAT:

If you see something you really love, and it seems like a pretty good deal, don't walk away… unless you're prepared to lose it.

SCHLEPPING STUFF:

No! Never let your booty become a burden when you're on the hunt. Most big markets have carts, even golf carts you can rent. But most savvy junkers bring their own transportation—shopping carts, laundry baskets, utility wagons, particularly the collapsible folding kind big enough for a worn-out child to take a nap in!

WHERE DID I SEE THAT? WHERE DID I LEAVE THAT?:

It's easy to lose your way at a big flea market. If you decide to leave something and go back and pick it up later, make sure you write down or even take a photo, not just of your loot, but of landmarks and booth numbers.

Opposite: On the hunt at the Rose Bowl Flea Market with booty cart in tow.

ONE ADMIS.

The Greatest

FLEA MARKET

on Earth

nd Sunday Every Month

.G.CANNING ATTRACTIONS

OSEBOWL   PASADENA

VOID WITH HOLE

13368865

GREEN

THE ART
OF THE HAGGLE

This is the situation—you are at the flea market, you have seen something you can't live without. You are ready to make it part of your life and collections', in other words—you want to buy it! How to proceed?

1. If there is a price on it, that's helpful. You know what the dealer wants to get for it. So you can start from there.

2. If there is not a price on it (more often than not this is the case!) then you have to start by asking, "What would you like for this?" Once the dealer has named a price, then the fun begins.

No self-respecting dealer ever really expects a buyer to consent to the named price, and rarely have I seen a sign on a dealer's table or booth or space saying, "Prices are non-negotiable!" If that was the case, they just took the fun out of the experience and I'd move on quickly. Haggling is the junker's sport, but there are certainly guidelines to how to do this. I always try to be respectful and avoid saying things like, "Are you kidding me? This isn't worth more than…." More than likely, I would start with "Is that the best you can do?" And sometimes it is and sometimes it isn't, but most dealers will offer you 10 percent off. Just to understand the dealer's point of view, I asked Mark Fogwell, a veteran of the Rose Bowl Flea Market, who started selling alongside his parents when he was eight. Here's what he had

to say: "The totality of bargaining is this—first of all, if you're polite, you can't do anything wrong, and if you're sincere, you can't do anything wrong. I am out there buying, too, and I've learned over the years to ask politely, 'Is that the best you can do?' I don't care if they lower the price or not, but it just keeps them happy and keeps everything OK.' Sometimes when we're traveling and going to low-budget flea markets, the dealer might say, 'Is $2 OK?' And I know it's worth much more than two bucks, so I'll say, 'Well, I only have a five dollar bill. Just take the five.' Sometimes I'm amazed that people will bargain with me when I say, 'I'll take a dollar,' and they say, 'How about 50 cents?'" That last thing Mark said is about the respect. I never ask for a better deal on something that is already priced very low. How could you bargain for something that's priced at a dollar? Sometimes you just know that the price is fair and you pay that. If you don't know, then shop around and see what similar objects are priced at. It's good to be informed and always good to haggle by the rules. Put yourself in the dealer's shoes! (More wisdom from Mark and his wife, Lorraine, on page 176.)

3. More is better and often cheaper: I've always found when shopping through a dealer's stall or space or shop never to ask the price of an individual item, but wait until you've gathered together all the things you're interested in, then ask. More than likely you'll get a better break.

From left to right: Haggling for polka-dot glasses—the more the better; adding another apron to my kitchen junk collection; considering a giant candle to add silly sparkle to the holidays; always be armed with lots of bags to haul the good stuff home.

THE ONE(S) THAT GOT AWAY

Obviously, there have been more than a few—paintings, chairs, a grandfather's clock, a blue rowboat—that got away for one reason or another: price, transportation challenges (being in London or Paris and falling in love with something not portable or too darn expensive to ship), indecision (seeing something, holding off for a quick circle around the market, deciding I have to have it, when boom! It's gone!). As the journey and the desire continue I've shifted my thinking to, "Que sera sera." In other words, if it was meant to be it will be! And, don't look back just because what you thought you couldn't live without is gone...maybe it's waiting for you right around the corner.

... AND ONE THAT DIDN'T!

I've always had a passion for collecting statues of the Infant of Prague. I guess it started when I was a devout little girl going to Mass and always passing a life-size version on my way out. Or perhaps it was because I loved the way many of these replicas are dressed with real robes and miniature crowns on their heads like the dolls I had always played with growing up. My obsession has built a collection of almost fifty or more, so it was not surprising that day I spotted the one seen opposite in one of my favorite shops in New Orleans that I pounced. I told my friend Maria, the proprietor of Antiques on Jackson, "He's mine!" What I didn't realize at the time was that this was a fifty-pound concrete baby that I would be trying to carry onto a plane the next day. "Never say never," I was thinking, as I dragged that baby Jesus through the New Orleans airport with a towel wrapped around his crowned head that wouldn't quite fit into my carry-on suitcase. "Will he get through security?" I thought, "and if not, what will they do with him? Will they erect an airport shrine surrounded by all the bottles of water and tubes of toothpaste and things that didn't quite follow TSA specifications?" I'll never forget waiting for the reaction of the inspectors as my blessed cargo went through the x-ray machine! Miracle of miracles, there was none and the next thing I knew I was winging my way home with my fifty-pound baby tucked securely in the overhead compartment.

Opposite: My fifty-pound Infant of Prague draped with strands of pom-poms, vintage necklaces, and sacred medals keeps watch over us in our city bedroom.

MARY
RANDOLPH CARTER

AN APARTMENT IS NOTHING BUT A BOX...

...that is until you fill it with all the stuff you love. After living in the same apartment for more than four decades, *Mary Randolph Carter* should know. She decided long ago there's always room for the things you've collected from the very first day until there's no more space! What? Never!

26

There are many joyful stages in the junker's journey.
First, there is the anticipation of the hunt, then the hunt itself, followed by the discovery of an object, the challenging haggle, the deal made, and finally the joy of bringing it home and making it part of your life.

For more than four decades I have found and made a home for so many of these loved objects in our New York City apartment twelve stories up with a slivered view (between two tall buildings) of Central Park and the roof garden of the Metropolitan Museum of Art. We, my husband, Howard, and I, moved in just before the birth of our first son, Carter, followed by his brother, Sam, three years later. Who knew after all this time we would still be here surrounded by so many of the same things we started out with—a step-back cupboard of pewter plates given to us by my parents as a wedding gift, two cricket tables found in an old tavern in Virginia, a rickety twig hat rack in the entrance hall weighted down with a lifetime collection of baseball hats, a banana clipboard and a matching yellow radio on top of an old pine windowpane cupboard, seen on page 36, in the kitchen. Hanging off a slightly listing partition of driftwood trap stakes in the center of our living room (seen on the previous page) are schools of hand-carved fish, a primitive watermelon sign, a fringed American flag, and a straw guitar. There are paintings galore, samplers, original children's artwork, pot holders and pincushions, painted furniture, dangling paper chains over the bed, and shelves and stacks of books, books, and more books.

Over time the two little boys grew up and left us with boxes of baseball cards stored in the tops of closets and a little cupboard (or two) filled with their childhood toys I couldn't bear to throw out. When I started to fall for flea market paintings, down came the sampler collection. When our beautiful old casement windows were replaced by a more efficient (ugly!) kind, I camouflaged them with peeling green shutters. (Seen on page 43.) Threadbare rugs—Orientals, Indians, ragged Raggs—have been replaced, but always with the same kind, never perfect.

Slowly, oh so slowly, these rooms have filled up with the essentials—not the sofas and chairs or a dining table, but the really essential things—the things we have collected, made, or been given that tell the stories of who we are. The things that make a home a home—a scrapbook of our living.

Previous page: In our living room, the trap stake partition divides the sitting and work areas. The serape-covered sofa is camouflaged with a collection of pillows and our grand-dog Cora. A pair of 3-D carnival plaques flank an embroidered interpretation of *Washington Crossing the Delaware* inspired by Emanuel Leutze's famous painting.

Opposite: My girlhood portrait oversees a bizarre mix of objects on a cricket table we've had since we first moved in!

Opening pages: A red painted hand on a cupboard with my initials points to a scrapbook wall of thrift shop art.

A HALLWAY GALLERY

Paintings are my obsession. And so, whenever I find an empty wall I create a little gallery of works of art to celebrate the junk masterpieces of the unknown artists that I collect. The exception in this exhibition in our city hallway is the large canvas by artist Tom Judd—a painting of two giant birds, a landscape and a blowup of a yearbook photo of his sister laid on top of vintage wallpapers. Surrounding it is a quartet of thrift shop finds—all originals, except the red tulips at lower left, which is a paint-by-numbers creation.

THE PECULIAR TOUCH

There are no rules when it comes to what you love and how you live with it! If you want to stick a weathered beach umbrella in your urban space far from any sandy beach, well, that's just fine! And if you find some really funky lamp in a thrift shop and pay $5 for it (or less!) and you know it's kind of hideous, but in that moment you find a peculiar beauty to it—then yes, go right ahead, put it in your living room, right next to the umbrella, the painting of the big lovable smiling Saint Bernard, and a really out-there valentine portrait on glass of boxing legend Joe Louis and his wife Marva—and let them live crazily-ever-after.

Opposite: It wasn't long after we moved into our apartment that I replaced the kitchen door with a pair of weathered green shutters, took out the metal cupboards above the sink and replaced them and others with a triple-decker of shelves. I wanted everything out in the open, not only for efficiency, but for the pure joy of gazing at all my yellow-ware bowls, plates, pot holders, tiles, trays, and even flea market artwork hanging (a bit hazardously) over the stove. The black-and-white checked shelf paper tacked above my collection of old enamel ladles makes a graphic backdrop for an exhibition of watercolors painted by my sister Cary of actual tools and toys. It also mimics the black-and-white tiles of the floor that live beneath our feet and the little primitive pine table (a bit wobbly after 40-some years) covered on top with a tropical oil cloth. As we all crowd around it, we count our blessings to have this cozy and cluttered eat-in kitchen with daylight streaming through a window framed by old barn wood.

Above: Our grand-dog Daisy matches the kitchen floor.

Top left: Uniformed guards—wine bottles from Portugal—stand at attention under a portrait of a ruffled gardener and atop a Bahamian painted fish.

Below left: To give my shelves more zip, I've strung Mexican Christmas cutouts that stay up all year!

On and below a ten-foot shelf running across our kitchen wall are treasures that I have accumulated over many years.

Take, for instance, the yellow radio that I flip on every morning to get me going; it's been there forever—in the same spot!

The matador wine bottle is a recent tenant, but not the dog biscuit jar created by my dog-loving brother Jimmie and Deborah, nor the strawberry cookie jar on its right. Up top to the far left is a little floral painted pitcher I carried back from London, a souvenir from a visit to Charleston Farmhouse, the home of the Bloomsbury group in the 1920s.

The surreal breakfast painting of fried eggs and bacon was a wondrous thrift shop find. The Mexican paper cutouts were tacked up for an engagement party three years ago and have never come down. The plate on the far left that reads "God Bless This Lousy Apartment" does not truly reflect the true feelings of those of us who have resided here for more than four decades.

Is clutter or an untidy home the true villain of our lives? Is it the enemy that we must rid ourselves of or could it be the very thing that saves us?

I have never met Marie Kondo, the author of *The Life-Changing Magic of Tidying Up: The Japanese Art of Decluttering and Organizing*, first published in the United States. in 2014, and since then according to the red sticker prominently displayed on the cover has sold three million copies, nor have I actually tried her world-famous KonMari method. I am not one of her thousands of "Konverts" as they call themselves. I first read about her in an article written by Taffy Brodesser-Akner ("Marie Kondo and the Ruthless War on Stuff") in the *New York Times* on July 6, 2016, but what really drew my attention was the oversize graphically illustrated headline—"STUFF" (one of my favorite words!) created out of hundreds of the everyday objects Kondo professes we must seek out and toss! Though

my first reaction is to poke fun and sneer a bit (as many have) at the concept of "tidying up," I must, in all fairness, share with you the very important first step in the KonMari method, which is to hold each item in your hands and ask, "Does this spark joy?" "If it does," she commands, "keep it." "If not, dispose of it." The idea is that the things we live with are meant to make us happy and, as she puts it, "speak to your heart." Therefore, if undecided about an object's fate try her "spark" test before you send it on its way.

Looking around at the hundreds of objects that clutter the shelves of my memory cupboard, at right, I wonder just how long the "spark" test would take? Substituting a quick visual grasp of each, in the focus of my eyes, I see sparks flying everywhere. I don't believe I would let go of anything except something functional like a stapler or tape dispenser, which do not hold me emotionally (they're sparkless), but go a long way in organizing my life. So in the end, I fear my cluttered cupboard would remain just as it is.

Kondo has actually taken this into account and suggests we save the mementos until the end of our journey. Her suggested sequence is clothes, then books, papers, and finally mementos. Perhaps, if I start the KonMari method in my clothes closet or in a drawerful of socks I might find some merit to it or as her book title reads, some "magic" in tidying up!

Opposite: So I won't forget, my memory cupboard is
stored with things—many of them given and made by family
and friends—that tell the stories of my life so far.

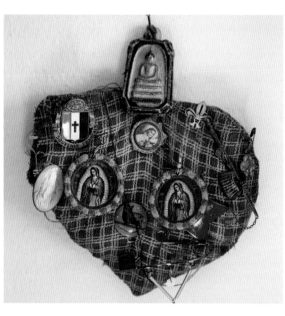

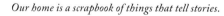

Our home is a scrapbook of things that tell stories.

Top row, left to right: *A heart-shaped pincushion of blessed totems; a weathered watch fob and a trio of ice cream spoons; Little Red Riding Hood and friends; a painting by outsider artist Sister Gertrude Morgan overlooks personal treasures and a head of a girl that my Mother said looked like me; two stylish monkey dolls;*

Middle row, left to right: *Ceramic pitchers; homage to King Elvis crowned with a halo of paper chains; a fishing boat made by an Outer Banks artist; a cubbyhole display;*

Bottom row, left to right: *A comfy armchair home to a sleepy terrier, a wide-awake bunny pillow resting on a hand-embroidered pillow of a dapper gentleman; favorite custom-made jewelry; tiny shells; a childhood portrait of my husband, Howard, and a Christmas tree, tiger painting, folkloric box, carved Native American, and a pair of mushrooms — concrete and papier-maché.*

ALWAYS MAKE ROOM FOR THINGS THAT MAKE YOU SMILE.
CARTER

"*Now I lay me down to sleep...*" began the little prayer I recited every night as a child kneeling next to my bed, cheating a little with crooked elbows propped atop the coverlets. In retrospect, those words were a little scary, yet, comforting, as I believed that angels watched over my sleep.

Perhaps, that is why I sleep so well these days lying in a bed my father made. It's essentially a headboard created out of one wide board secured with a pair of pine trap stakes rescued from the waters of the river near our house in Virginia. The canopy of colorful construction paper chains, made many years ago (and often replaced!) by my niece Mary Randolph dangles over a framed piece of a flowery pink chenille bedspread. The mix of Indian coverlets topping a feathery comforter change from season to season. Desperate for more storage space, the perfectly-sized drawers for storing socks, scarves and under garments (ooh là là!), and extra shelves for books, seemed the perfect solution. Taking a look at the mountain of bedside reading stacked near by, it clearly did not meet the challenge. Three pairs of old shutters add a slightly romantic barrier to the city noise below while camouflaging a trio of efficient but very unaesthetic windows.

Tiny Treasures

Above: Lighting the way for the lucky guest who sleeps in our cozy guest room is one of the weirder lamps I've ever collected, constructed out of a rusty can and rubber ball. The artist doll sporting a straw hat and a chic striped T-shirt is definitely French. The caged songbirds sing a wakeup call to sleepyheads when a button is pressed.

Top right: A shelf of tiny treasures hangs on our bedroom wall. Up top, an altar of blessed icons lined up before a Mexican votive painting on tin floats above a collection of miniature books, a Thumbelina-size green teapot, itsy-bitsy shells, a fragile wooden swan, a Palm Sunday flower, Mutt and Jeff pitchers, and in the center, a double-door home to a Lilliputian couple.

Below right: Instead of hiding them away, I nestle my collection of Mexican religious bracelets in a tarnished bowl rimmed with little fake gems for all to enjoy.

Opposite: A great way to save and savor your children's childhood artifacts is to display them in a charming cupboard. This one hanging on the wall of the bedroom that our two sons grew up in is filled with some of their favorite childhood books, and Gumby and a little golden Cub Scout share guard duties. When wound up, the seemingly never weary little Pierrot dances to the tinkling tune that beguiled our boys long ago…and still does!

I'm not sure why I chose to build our bookshelves right in the path of the sun that lights them up and continues to fade their spines year after year. Other than the large sombrero shading a dozen or so volumes, nothing is protected. Even the family photographs that have become part of the exhibit are slowly turning sepia. What can I do? Close the shutters, perhaps? Drape them with a burlap curtain? No! No! It's far too late. They'll just continue to bake as I sit in my multicolored Adirondack chair, at right, basking in the glow of another day enjoying this hefty collection of books dating from my college days and a quirky display of artwork, including a paper-mâché dinosaur in blue made by my son Carter in third grade. On the bench before them is a velvety replica of Elvis and a one-of-a-kind Merry-Go-Round Prayer Wheel decorated with Christmas bulbs.

Tip: Use your bookshelves to display much more than books. Mixing in photographs, paintings, and artwork adds lots more character.

BUFFY BIRRITTELLA

HOME IS WHERE YOUR HORSE IS

Make room in your home for all the things that you love. That goes for family and friends, dogs and cats, and, in *Buffy Birrittella's* case—horses, too! From the age of eight she knew she wanted to be a cowgirl, but this cowgirl from New York City did something about it. She made her way out to the West and found a way to resource and preserve a homemade life.

SUNDANCE

I ALWAYS WANTED TO BE A COWGIRL. IT STARTED ON A PONY RIDE IN YONKERS, BUT IT REALLY HAPPENED YEARS LATER IN SUNDANCE.
BUFFY

Home is where
Your horse is.

How does a little girl who grew up in Yonkers, New York, a little scared of horses, dream of being a cowgirl and then become a collector of the very thing that terrified her the most? And that's not just the wooden kind seen on the previous page in her log house in Utah, but real horses named Cheyenne, Scout, Dakota, Cochise, and Lola. Maybe it started with the summertime pony rides at her grandmother's house on the Hudson and then, much later, hitching her career to that of a young designer named Ralph Lauren (forty-eight years ago!), who eventually sent her to the set of *The Great Gatsby* to assist in styling his men's collection on the male cast and its leading man, Robert Redford. The summer after the film wrapped, Redford invited her along with other *Gatsby* pals to visit his Sundance ranch. That was the summer Buffy Birrittella learned to ride, beat her fear of horses, and added that dream role of cowgirl to her life. Those real cowgirl roots began to thrive years later when she bought her own little cabin at Sundance and started to fill it with the kinds of western things she had already been mixing with her more Americana collections of log cabin quilts and Shaker baskets in her apartment and office in New York City. That love of homemade things was instilled in her by her mother's mother who came to this country from rural Czechoslovakia when she was a girl. "My grandmother grew up creating and making things," recalls Buffy. "My grandfather

was the same—always crafting." Those handmade clothes and objects were the things they cherished and so, as time went by, did she. All of a sudden, the Native American baskets, the weavings, the rugs, the trading blankets, the Edward Curtis photographs framed in tramp art frames, the turquoise jewelry, beaded moccasins, the painted furniture, and every imaginable type of horse artifact had found a true home. In the winter of 1996, riding up a ski lift at Sundance, a friend pointed out a big log house that was up for sale. By then her little cabin was bulging (with more stuff in storage), and on top of that her horses (who had been boarded in other people's stables) were clamoring for digs of their own. Believing what the sign reads on the opposite page, "Home is where your horse is," she wasted no time, bought the house, moved in, built a corral and tack house for the horses, a tree house for guests, a billiards room to gather in with friends, and, of course, a place for all the things—collected and given—that make this cowgirl happy and longing for more!

Previous page: A little carved wooden horse might have come from a saddle-maker's shop, outfitted with a perfect bridle, miniature saddle, and serape blanket. The hickory chair he stands on is softened with pillows made from remnants of faded trading blankets. The hand-painted deerskin branded with her initials "BB" in a heart was a gift.

Opposite from top left: A favorite weathered hat; Buffy and a colt by Andrea Dern; corraled with Palmomina Paint Lola; signature turquoise; her mantra captured on a sign made by her horsekeeper friend Glade Collard; a treat for Lola; a childhood pony ride.

*Above: Buffy's tree house is a fantasy refuge for friends
and family built from recycled materials.*

*Top: The old green-painted and antlered A-shaped shelf
decorated with horse heads (what else?) welcomes guests
at the entrance of the tree house.*

*Bottom: An American flag stuck in a barrel of
wildflowers at the main entrance signals that the cowgirl
of the house is in residence.*

Tip: Building a house or adding onto an existing one can be the ultimate test of your collector's resourcefulness. If you love the look of "lived-in," start by combing local salvage yards not only for the basic building materials, but also for everything from doors to doorknobs. See the *Junker's Guide* for some of our collectors' favorites.

HOW TO BUILD OLD INTO NEW: THE GREEN ART OF SALVAGING

One summer on a hot sleepless night, Buffy decided she needed to build a sleeping porch cooled by outside breezes. That simple idea morphed into her three hundred-square-foot tree house, seen opposite, built by local craftsmen under the direction of Jeffrey Cayle. Almost all the materials were sourced and recycled from the area. The pegged barn wood siding came from two barns that were being dismantled, the trestle wood floor (see following page) salvaged from the Great Salt Lake Railroad, is naturally fire-retardant because of the salt content left after water evaporation. "Not one tree was cut down for this project!" Buffy insists. The great posts that lift it thirty feet into the trees were sourced locally from land that had been cleared. The old red door, light fixture, and the rusty galvanized roof of the tack house, at right, were hunted down at salvage yards.

Above: The recycled red door of the tack house matches a red "B" for Buffy and the red tractor seat of a put-together stool, a gift from the author. Inside are saddles, horse tack, treats, and oats. To the left of the door is another horse collectible, a portrait of a horse on wood, a gift from Buffy's friend Andrea Dern.

Left: On the trail to Buffy's house, a view of the Wasatch Mountains. In winter, she can ski right to her door!

What makes Buffy happiest is sharing the things that she loves with the people she loves. It's what makes collecting meaningful to her. "It's not only about creating an environment that is special and unique to you," she says, "but sharing it with friends and family." What better evidence than the way she shares the most comfortable old iron bed layered with umpteen pillows (many made from remnants of old Navajo rugs and blankets) and a long bolster at the back so it doubles as a sofa; an outrageous view from a balcony just outside with soothing breezes, the rustle of trees, and occasionally the soft clatter of rain on the old tin roof; and most of all her collections personally placed from floor to ceiling on the recycled wooden beams, shelves, nooks, and branches sprouting from her lovingly homemade hideaway floating in the trees.

Left: Custom-made by a Montana artisan, a hand-crafted chandelier of antlers (collected in the wild) lit by electrified oil lamps floats just above barn-siding shelves curated with Edward Curtis photographs and Native American baskets. Below are all manner of reutilized objects—a blue shoe polish box next to the bed, a cowhide–covered trunk coffee table, a funky twig rocking chair, a pair of pressed-back oak chairs, and if you search very carefully—a little red carved devil next to the door!

Following pages: Overlooking a trestle table desk littered (perfectly) with Buffy treasures, including a tramp art framed Curtis photograph, an old leather cargo box, bark frames, and a pair of oil lamps, is a primitive painting of a noble white horse discovered in Great Barrington, Massachusetts (on a junking trip with me!). Lined up in front is a children's cast iron Native American village bookended on the far left by a very rare Anasazi pottery ladle bought at auction and on the other end by a an old camera in a worn leather case.

More Is Better. Buffy's Roundup of Horse Collectibles

Top row: A needlepoint pillow portrait of Buffy's first horse, Cheyenne; tabletop painting of Buffy on Cheyenne by Andrea Dern; galloping metal matchbox case; a sketch of "Buffy's Horse" as seen by a young horse lover; to celebrate this special gift—an old metal relief of a cowboy astride his horse, Buffy had it embedded in an exterior stone wall;

Middle row: A hand-painted horse tray; a prehistoric Anasazi pottery canteen decorated with a primitive horse on both sides; one of a pair of old brass bookends haloed by a vintage Apache basket; a blue horse windmill weight surrounded by antlers;

Bottom row: Beaded Native American moccasins; a cast-iron horse used as a doorstop; bucking Bronco detail on a hand-forged fire screen; portrait of a horse in wood hangs next to the tack house door; a folk art painting of a long-tailed dancing horse given to Buffy by yours truly.

COLLECT-BY-COLOR

One easy way to build a collection is to fall in love with one color like Buffy did long ago—we call it "Buffy Blue." Whether it was an old blue pie safe or a pair of beaded cowgirl gloves, or moccasins, or turquoise earrings—she had to have them! Pick your color and display all shades of it together or artfully punctuate your home with it room by room.

A MODERN TOUCH

Giving a modern touch to a vintage blue pie safe filled with workout clothes and pool towels, Buffy curated a trio of disparate objects—a Native American woven storage basket and a bleached-out horse skull on a stand against her graphic photograph of the Church at San Ildefonso, Pueblo, New Mexico.

Tip: Don't be afraid to mix contemporary art and objects with vintage furniture or vice versa—vintage objects and paintings in a modern space. The mix will give each period a singular style.

Above: Buffy spotted this vintage blue pie safe in the Maine Antique Digest, *a monthly must-read for serious collectors.*

Top right: Fit for a rodeo queen, Buffy lassoed this vintage pair at the Indian Market held each August in Santa Fe.

FASHION AS ART

Don't hide your beautiful accessories in a drawer or closet. Take, for example, the vintage pair of fringed beaded gloves, seen opposite. When Buffy's not wearing them, she stuffs them with paper and displays them on a cast iron stand. Same goes for her collection of beaded moccasins, a blue favorite seen below. They spend their leisure time lined up on a shelf until she has the urge to wear them.

A CHORUS LINE

Tiny fragile objects like the beautiful earrings from Buffy's western collection seen at right should never be jammed into a jewelry box where they are fated to get separated or helplessly tangled. Why not share them like little works of art hanging from a piece of deerskin?

Left: A well-worn pair of Buffy's beaded moccasins made after the originals by Native American tribes and found in a shop in Santa Fe.

Above: *Buffy's love of blue--turquoise earrings dangling with others from a thin piece of deerskin.*

Sometimes a memory of a place is so strong it provokes the desire to re-create it filled with specific things that might bring back that experience. Buffy's billiards room was provoked by such a memory—playing pool with her dad, her brother, and friends in the family billiards room in her childhood home in Park Hill, Yonkers. Furnished with a vintage pool table from the legendary Blatt's in New York City, and equipped with a bar and a mega-sized eighty-five-inch flat screen TV, it had the basic trappings of what had been. What hadn't been was a major stone fireplace, floor-to-ceiling shelves filled with her collections of Native American baskets and Curtis photographs, a banquette covered with a vintage bearskin and layers of pillows recycled from early worn-out rugs, and the bold red and black pattern of a Navajo rug over the fireplace that found its way from the mudroom floor to the back of a chair, and then to its present place of honor. "In fact, most things in the room," she recalls, "seemed to have found their way here from other places in the house."

Above: Buffy's furry pal Cherokee stalks hummingbirds from the edge of a serape-covered table.

Top left: An Indiana hickory loveseat brightened with pillows made from the remnants of an old Pendleton blanket with a Beacon Mills blanket folded over the back.

Bottom left: A little rag doll dressed Buffy style in a plaid shirt and fringed leather pants.

Bottom right: Early rag rugs like this one of a horse-to-horse greeting are better preserved as wall hangings rather than displayed underfoot.

Opposite: The telltale signs of a horse collector abide outside Buffy's Sundance home—a horse sign made by a local friend, the "eyedazzler" saddle blanket, the worn cowboy hat, the horse head and hoof on her Santa Fe-made boots, even the boot jack features a tiny horse.

Perfectly Patched

There's more than one way to save an old rug, particularly one as meaningful to the owner as the beautiful red Navajo seen here. It was Buffy's first, bought around 1980 (from M. Finkel & Daughter, Philadelphia) and when she placed it on the most trodden place in her previous cabin—the kitchen floor—it got, according to her, "worn, torn, and abused." To save what was left she folded it up and put it away until she moved into her new house. That's when she decided to give it a new life, patched by a local rug whisperer of sorts with pieces from rugs and skins and fabrics that didn't make it. Now it lies on a floor with less foot traffic, but as you can see some of her patches need patches.

P.S. If patches aren't your thing consider re-cycling your rugs and blankets into unique pillow covers and the like. Be sure to save all the remnants for future projects.

Everyone knows that Brimfield (in Brimfield, Massachusetts) is to a junker like the Triple Crown is to racing—three times a year (May, July, and September) for five days straight. (For more details go to Brimfieldshow.com) Whenever I told my junker friends I had never been to Brimfield, they were aghast! How could it be that that the 'Queen of Junk' had never hunted the junker's mecca? My wimpy answer was always the same, "Gee, something always came up!" That was until a sweltering Friday in July 2016 when I finally made it to the junker's promised land.

◆LOCATION◆
MASSACHUSETTS

BRIMFIELD
MARKET

I think from all the stories I'd heard about this legendary market—hundreds of dealers set up over acres of fields, and thousands of ravenous collectors storming the gates to get to the good stuff first—I was downright intimidated! I also thought for my first visit I would have to tag along with a veteran. Well, that was I thought, until I actually experienced Brimfield for myself, along with my son Carter and daughter-in-law Kasia, seen below. Though July is the hottest time for a first visit it turned out to be kind of a plus, making it less crowded and easier to navigate.

DON'T LEAVE
SOMETHING BEHIND
THAT YOU LOVE.
CHANCES ARE
YOU'LL NEVER
SEE IT AGAIN.
CARTER

Brimfield was much cozier than I thought it would be. There's basically one street that goes through town with dealers set up in fields on either side. Though veterans have a total strategy in place—which dealers, in which fields, on what days. Perhaps, since I knew nothing and had no grand scheme, I was just a happy junker with no pressure. I spent one whole day hunting in one market and was totally happy. Look around on these pages and you'll spy some of my treasures of the day. One of the goofiest was the glass jar filled with abandoned wasp's nests.

That's me (below) with my Brimfield buddy, Randy Siciliano, known as the "Jersey Picker" because that's where he's from and where he started picking in 1992. Randy's legendary especially at Brimfield where he's been a colorful character since 1997! On the hunt from one flea market to another all year–round, he reckons he sets up at close to thirty a year. With experience like this he has wisdom to share…See Randy's Golden Rules of Junk below…

FIRST TIME I WENT
I DISCOVERED
THIS ISN'T ANY OLD
ROCK CONCERT.
THIS ONE IS
WOODSTOCK!
RANDY

Randy's Golden Rules of Junk

1. Be cautious what you throw out—everything has a market.

2. Never buy in the dark.

3. Education never comes cheap. You'll make mistakes, but learn from them.

4. It's not the buyer's job to educate the seller.

5. The word *worth* can be dangerous in the antiques world. An object's worth evolves every time it changes hands.

71

RENÉE PARKER WERNER

BRINGING THE OUTSIDE INSIDE

Once she fell in love with Anne Hathaway's cottage in Stratford-upon-Avon and Monet's gardens at Giverny, it wasn't long before *Renée Parker Werner* went about creating her own. When she found her secret garden wall behind the charred remains of a romantic old house in New Orleans, she put on her garden gloves and went to work.

"It was like the rising of the phoenix from the ashes." Which is quite literally true given that the house she bought twenty years ago had been mysteriously razed by fire with no walls standing except the front facade. She had just retired from a lifetime career (thirty-two years!) as a stewardess for Delta Airlines and decided she would give up the perfect little home (close to the airport) she had created surrounded by herb gardens and climbing roses inspired by Anne Hathaway's cottage outside of Stratford-upon-Avon, and be closer to friends that lived in town. One of those friends, hearing that she wanted something very different from her charming cottage with a little land for a garden, took her to a shady street in the Lower Garden District and stood her before a two-story balconied wooden house circa 1850. "When I first saw it," she recalls, "there wasn't even a front door—just a piece of plywood nailed over the opening. There was a lock on it which was really silly since all you had to do was walk around the back where it was all open. It was like a stage set with only the front facade intact." It had been empty for three years. "The pigeons," she chuckles, "just flew in and out." When she walked into the burned-out front hallway she knew exactly what she would do. The clues left by the remains of the interior would guide her to return it to the exact way it had been in 1850. But it wasn't until she walked into the tangled garden behind the house and saw the astonishing brick wall rising at its end, that she really knew that she had to find a way to make this piece of earth hers. Already she was asking herself, "How can I design a garden that will relate to that wall?" And, once it was hers, that's what she did. She commissioned an iron rose arbor inspired this time not by Anne Hathaway, but by Claude Monet and her many visits to his masterpiece gardens at Giverny. "I had to start small planting everything fragrant—gardenia, boxwood, roses. Every year my Christmas tree would be a tree to plant in the garden—a sweet olive tree or a calamondin orange or a bay tree." Though it wasn't "instant gratification," as she puts it, today some of her bays are over fourteen feet tall. She attributes their amazing growth to the ash in the soil, one of the few benefits of the fire.

It was two years before she could sleep in the house. Luckily, a dear friend who had helped her transform her former tract house into an English cottage and who was totally opposed to her buying this one, finally changed his mind and even handcrafted the staircase in the front hall that had initially horrified him. Her neighbors thought that a little angel had landed there. And they were right.

Previous pages: Weathered green shutters open from the front hall into the kitchen.

Left: An almost human-size Mary watches over the front hallway. The doors open to the newly added garden room.

HOW TO BUILD YOUR ORANGERY (OR JUST THE SPIRIT OF ONE!)

Sometimes it takes just one thing, like Renée's beautiful old porthole window, seen at left, to inspire a whole room, or just the look of it. Renée's was built mostly of salvaged windows and doors she had stock-piled for years. All the hardware is mismatched and all the minimal furnishing, including the bracketed shelf made out of a split cypress tree, were flea-market finds.

Did you know?

An orangery was a sun-flooded room or annex appended to elegant homes from the seventeenth to nineteenth centuries, built to protect orange or other citrus trees from winter's frost.

Opposite: Pristine, sun-flooded garden room is a spare contradiction to the rest of Renée's treasure-packed home.

Above: A skeleton of a chair camouflaged with a drapey piece of burlap.

Top right: Renée and I enjoy a visit in her orangery. For years she stockpiled the salvaged doors and windows that open up to the sweet fragrance of her garden.

Bottom right: Bittersweet, Renée's Yorkshire Terrier, her "most precious treasure of all," named for the way she sees life.

FOR ME, IT'S ALWAYS BEEN ABOUT THE GARDEN. FIRST THE GARDEN THEN THE HOUSE.
RENÉE

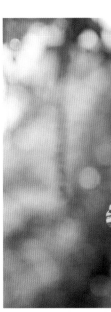

Maybe Renée's love of gardening started with her great grandmother, a Tasha Tudor look-alike and nurturer who would take her as a child through her garden in Thawville, Illinois (population: 250), sharing the stories of all her bulbs and what they yielded through the seasons. Or maybe it was the inspiration of those gardens in Europe she explored many years later, that truly turned her thumbs green and her heart palpitating to create her own. "For me it has always been about the garden. First the garden, then the house," she declares surrounded by her secret garden of sweet olive, boxwood, gardenia, climbing roses, elephant ears, Egyptian papyrus, orange and lemon trees, and French bay laurels that have grown to fourteen feet since she planted them twenty years ago.

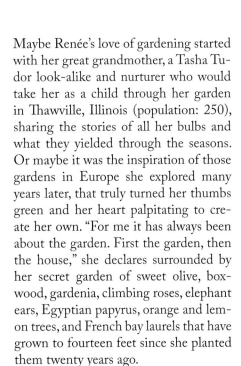
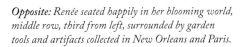

Opposite: Renée seated happily in her blooming world, middle row, third from left, surrounded by garden tools and artifacts collected in New Orleans and Paris.

When Renée dug into the huge weed pile in the back of her house she discovered a mountain of old crumbling bricks. "Well, that's my kitchen floor," she thought. And to make it happen she lugged, sorted, and got down on her knees to lay it out like a life-size puzzle of broken bits and pieces. When it was finished she saw that it was the perfect pathway out to the garden beyond and to the ancient brick wall at its end that had first inspired her love of this magical place. (For more on collecting old bricks and flooring, see the following pages.)

The centerpiece of the kitchen is the almost seven-foot Spanish trestle table with carved legs and a twisted iron base. Though the provenance of the six leather upholstered chairs, each with a gold monogram on their upper right side, is unknown, they are distinctly French in design. The mantelpiece to its right was saved from the fire and left in its blackened state. The intricate plaster piece above it was found in a French flea market. A kitchen mascot, "Lamby," perched atop a solid wooden armoire that stores Renée's collections of mismatched china, was a gift from a good friend. "Old houses," she reminds us, "have no closets so armoires and hooks are very important."

Did you know?
The French armoire, usually a two-door, often carved, wooden closet with shelves, dates back to before the sixteenth century. Before the twentieth century most homes didn't have closets. Clothes were stored in cabinets, wardrobes, and dressers; or, if you weren't rich enough, your clothes were hung on hooks or pegs.

RESCUING OLD SHUTTERS

The only real doors Renée has in her house are the ones that survived the fire—a charred pair that slide together to divide the front parlor from the kitchen. The rest are all shutters, wonderfully mismatched with lots of louvers missing, but she loves that and is drawn to their wonderful disrepair and their "time-worn look." When she started putting her house together twenty years ago, she had no money and would comb the salvage yards where "things would speak to her." She'd pick up what she could afford, finding the heights to fill the doorways upstairs and downstairs. A handy friend who put them together for her would say, "They don't match!" And, she'd say, "But that's what I love about them."

Above: A vintage pair of arched louvered shutters were cut down to fit and romanticize a storage space under a high-backed porcelain farm sink.

Top, right: Peekaboo shutters allow a view from the hall into the kitchen. The only thing perfect about them is their height. (See a full view on page 73.)

WHERE TO HUNT

Drive into almost any junk or salvage yard and you'll be welcomed by armies of shutters. Their multitudes mean bargains for you!

Tip: Write window measurements down and stick them in your wallet. You never know when you'll see a stack of shutters on the side of the road. I always go for the taller ones as you can cut them down to size. Like Renée, I don't mind if they're missing slats (cheaper those), but if that's not your thing, buy an extra one with same-size slats to fill in what's missing. Flaking paint can be solved by taking a sturdy wire brush or steel wool to it, then hosing it off, air drying, and spraying on paint or a clear matte sealant. To dust between the slats spray on a furniture polish and swipe a Swiffer duster. Or just use a soft cloth and mild detergent.

Left: Since the pair of red shutters didn't fill the doorway, Renée filled the gap by hinging on a distant cousin in green.

Above: Old houses never have enough closets so Renée customized one for her bedroom out of a trio of very tall shutters leaving room on top for her collection of vintage luggage, trunks, and travel cases.

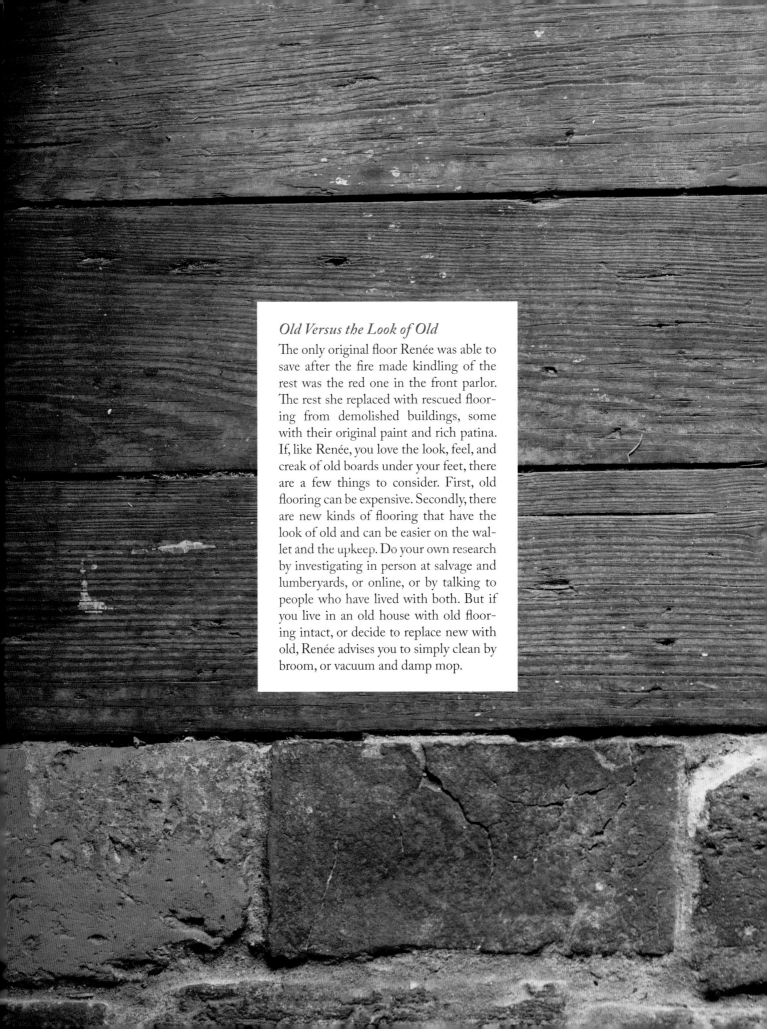

Old Versus the Look of Old

The only original floor Renée was able to save after the fire made kindling of the rest was the red one in the front parlor. The rest she replaced with rescued flooring from demolished buildings, some with their original paint and rich patina. If, like Renée, you love the look, feel, and creak of old boards under your feet, there are a few things to consider. First, old flooring can be expensive. Secondly, there are new kinds of flooring that have the look of old and can be easier on the wallet and the upkeep. Do your own research by investigating in person at salvage and lumberyards, or online, or by talking to people who have lived with both. But if you live in an old house with old flooring intact, or decide to replace new with old, Renée advises you to simply clean by broom, or vacuum and damp mop.

Bricks Underfoot

Many old kitchen floors were made of brick to prevent fires caused by flying embers from open hearth cooking. That was not Renée's main intention, but the minute she discovered the pile of old bricks hidden in her back garden she knew immediately they would become her kitchen floor. Without such a resource at hand, there are plenty of places to find bricks or brick pavers (slightly thinner) that have the look and character of those that Renée found. Just search for old bricks online and you'll find an array of places that offer up the look of distressed and antiqued bricks for floors, walls, or even just a backsplash! Renée cleans her beautiful old bricks the same way she cleans her old floors—with a hearty sweep or vacuum and a swish over with a damp mop.

THE ART OF THE UNFRAMED

RESCUING JUNK MASTERPIECES

I love the charm of a little grime ("patina," I call it!) on my paintings. But even I occasionally try to brighten up what Howard calls my "dark paintings." Below are some ideas on how to go about it, plus how to deal with rips and tears and some general cosmetic improvisations. Proceed at your own risk!

Don't do too much. Most paintings are pretty fragile. If you must, barely dampen a soft cloth and try to lightly remove surface dust and grime with it. Too much soap and water will dry out and crack the pigments. Never use any spray cleaner on an old painting.

Dry clean an oil painting using my mother's Wonder Bread method. Ball up very fresh Wonder Bread slices into doughy little pellets. Rub one at a time over the surface of the painting.

To repair a small tear or rip (I say, "Why bother?") carefully place a snippet of duct tape on the back of the painting, behind the tear. This should help it cosmetically and also help to prevent further damage. Duct tape comes in colors now so pick one that blends in. Another fix is to attach a fine piece of linen on the back, over the tear, using a white glue.

Touchup a painting with markers or crayons. For watercolors, try Caran d'Ache, Swiss-made crayons that when dipped in water give a watercolor effect.

Renée recalls how the dealers of the French flea markets and *brocante* shops would look at her when she bought an old tattered painting with a hole in it and ask, "Pourquoi?" "They just couldn't understand why I would want something so damaged. It was, of course, because I could afford it," she says. "If it hadn't been tattered or had no hole, I never would have been able to." Buying them unframed was cheaper still, and there was something about that unfettered style that appealed to her. So she hung them exactly as she found them—unframed.

Left: A cluster of Renée's unframed paintings with tattered edges and crackled patina hangs in her kitchen. Floral and kitchen still lifes are her favorite, and anything that conjures up her life in Paris like the Van Gogh-inspired "Starry Night" at the bottom.

CREATE A MOOD

There's something about Renée's front parlor that feels a bit like a haunted Roman ruin. Perhaps it's the monumental twelve-foot-tall fluted column of heavy cast iron decorated with an acanthus leaf motif that took two strong men to heave into its corner resting place? Renée loves the way it looks leaning artistically like a fallen relic of another age next to a similarly distressed cast iron urn atop an old weathered pedestal.

PAINT IT BLUE

Except for the wall left behind the seven-foot mirror rising above the cast iron fireplace and mantel (a gift from a friend honoring Renée's courage to restore St. Mary), all the original plaster walls were destroyed by the fire. Instead of crying over what was lost Renée chose to go a little crazy by painting the new walls an exotic blue, an incredible backdrop for the wonderful hodgepodge of things she's gathered there.

CURATE A COLLECTION

Look for a way to comingle objects with the same vibe or story. Renée's collection of palettes displayed together on the table at left is a perfect little paint-spattered exhibit.

MIKE WOLFE

PICKING & PRESERVING AMERICA'S STORIES

It started when *Mike Wolfe* was just a boy spying things in the garbage that seemed worth saving—like the bicycle he never had. From there it grew into a real live treasure hunt, all across America, picking through the overflow of people's lives, and discovering that everything has a meaningful story.

Picture this little kid, age four, in Joliet, Illinois, finding his way to his kindergarten class a block away from his house, meandering through back alleyways to avoid being picked on by the big kids. Along the way he'd see old men tinkering in their garages. He remembers going into these spaces and being fascinated by all the things hanging from ceilings. And then there were the stories they would share with him. Stories about a cigar box or their tools or just about their lives. That little kid was named Mike Wolfe and that childhood fascination with people, their stuff, and their stories became the inspiration for his eight-year-old phenomenal hit cable show 'American Pickers.' But back to the alleys... when garbage day came around little Mike was always picking through it. He was intrigued by what people were throwing out. One day he saw a balloon tire bicycle in the garbage. Being raised by a single mom struggling to provide for him and his older sister and younger brother, he never had a bike. So when he saw that bike, he said, "Wow, I've got to grab this!" And after that he kept pulling them out, sometimes just pieces and parts of them, so that by the time he was five he was a bike collector. "My collecting started with exploring. Whether in a junkyard or an alley or just walking down the street and looking into someone's garbage. When you're a child you want to explore and discover. You want to search, you're curious,

and that's why I started collecting."

And then his mother did the most amazing thing! She gave him the garage so he had a place to not only store his bikes and whatever other stuff he brought home, but a place to work on it all. But, ultimately it was the bikes that were his real passion. He was fascinated by their movement and the design, but mainly how he felt when he rode them. For him bicycles represented his first real sense of freedom, and from that time until now they have been at the center of his life—riding them, building them, collecting them, selling them (eventually in his own bike shops), discovering other things in the search for them, trading them, and then, when he was in his mid-twenties, he walked out on the field of the world's largest antique motorcycle swap right in his own town of Davenport, Iowa, and discovered vintage bikes and motorcycles (for the first time!) and his collecting life was changed forever. He closed up his bike shop, sold all his inventory, and went on the road to discover and pick.

Previous pages: Ready to ride—a trio of Mike's vintage motorcycles (a blue 1938 Harley Knucklehead; red and black 1939 Harley Knucklehead) and a rusty relic—a 1932 Ford roadster that works almost as well as the vintage Mobilgas pump.

Opposite: Vintage cast iron and enamel car emblems or badges were originally attached to grilles, hoods, and trunk lids like distinctive jewelry.

Following pages: A special visit with Mike inside the "Mike Cave," his 2000-square-foot museum/garage and private home of the King of Bikes' personal best.

Above: Mike attached the cast iron skull symbol found on a convent door onto this green industrial table showcasing a rare Koslow racing engine circa 1930, flanked by what looks like a terra-cotta Buffalo nickel, and a pair of skull taillights circa 1928. Left: The iconic Indian Motorcycle logo emblazoned on the tank of a 1939 four-cylinder model parked in Mike's garage.

Below: Mike shows off a shoeshine sign from the late '20s discovered on an American Pickers pick in New York City.

Top right: A blue trunk that once stored sample tires supports a collection of gas-powered model tether cars from the 1930s. Each car is tethered to a central post as it races around a miniature track at speeds upwards of two hundred miles per hour.

Below right: Mike loves the colors of this late 1920s plaster cigar store replica of a proud Native American brave.

If you're a motorcycle enthusiast then you know that a knucklehead is a retronym referring to a Harley Davidson engine. But if, like me, you are unschooled (a total dummy, to be exact!) in this particular field, then you would not know that the quartet of industrial-looking objects displayed in Mike Wolfe's off-the-charts cycle-crazy garage are exactly that—knucklehead engines! Vintage Knuckleheads like these beauties from circa 1936 to '47 are gold to a motorcycle collector so even disemboweled they are treated as such. Mike sees them as art and until they are eventually reassembled into working cycles again, he will exhibit them as such. Beneath them is displayed another work of motor art—a 1920s chain-driven pedal car—an elaborate toy for a very lucky child. In this case, Mike, or perhaps his lucky six-year-old daughter, Charlie!

Following pages: Most of the great motor signs were created as advertising for products like Oilzum Motor Oil, one of the first American motor oils, introduced in 1905. Today, signs with bold graphics like this are found more often decorating an apartment wall than the outside a garage.

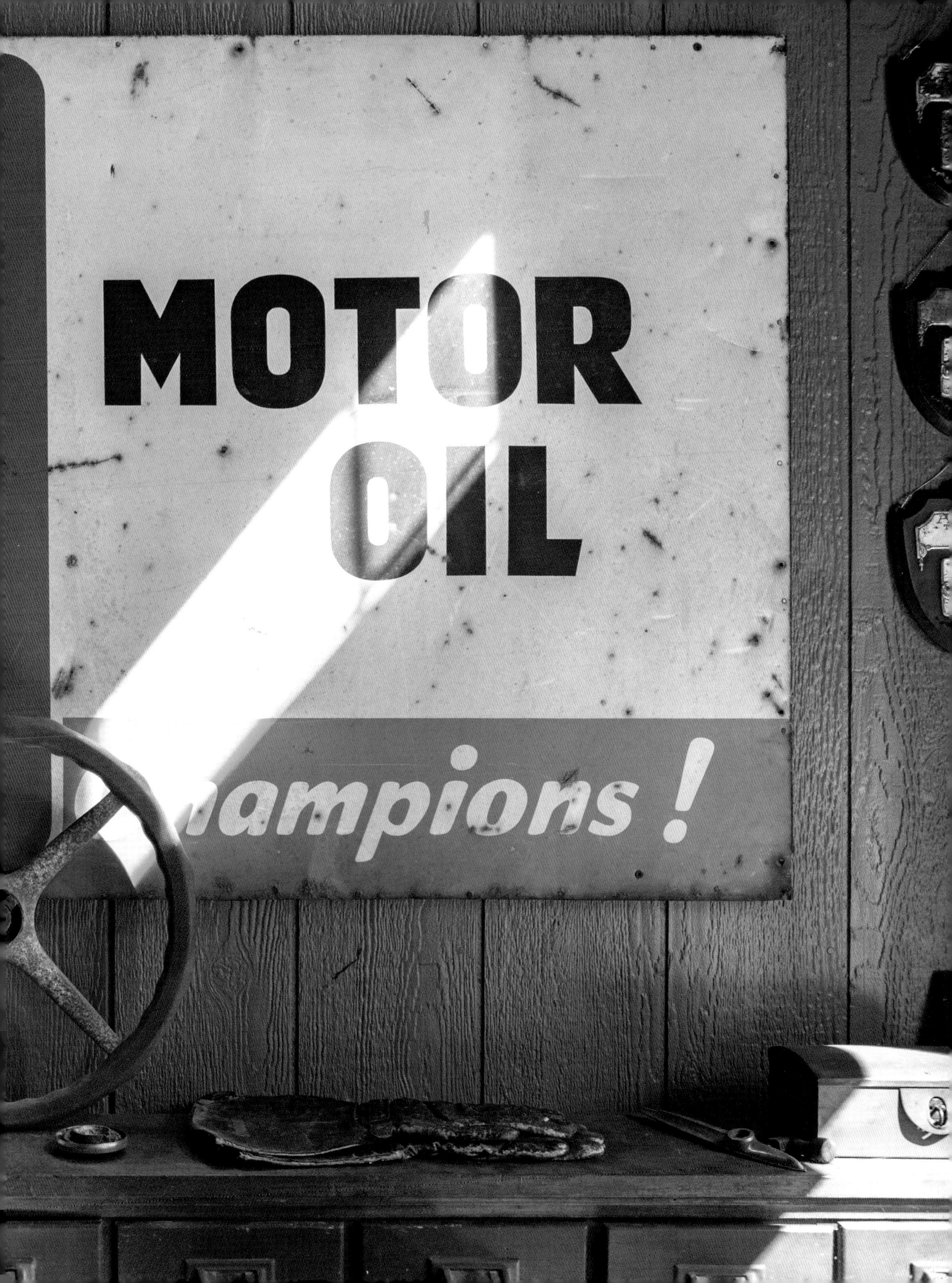
MOTOR
OIL
hampions !

Signed, Sealed and Delivered

If you watch *American Pickers*, then you know how much Mike Wolfe loves signs—the bolder the better, the rustier the better! The only condition is that they message his favorite passion—the world of transportation. He admits that when he started collecting signs he could only afford the ones that were pretty roughed up with rust and dirt. Today he appreciates all that wear and tear. As he puts it, "When something is broken down, beat up, baked, rusted, and faded it continues the story." The Faisle hi-wheel bike seen under the Mobil sign, top row, center, is another story he loves. "No reason not to hang something as rare and beautiful as this on your wall," he says.

IT'S NOT ABOUT THE PIECE, IT'S ABOUT THE JOURNEY, AND MOST OF ALL— THE STORIES.
MIKE

Don't we all wish we had a garage that looked like Mike's private warehouse? All collectors yearn for a space to exhibit their wares, but more than likely we are confined to showing off our stuff on shelves, cupboards, or walls. Which is fine, but if you are lucky enough to have a garage or barn, a shed or chicken coop that's more than likely jammed with stuff, consider cleaning it out to show off your collections.

Mike's corrugated steel space has been beautifully finished with poured concrete floors, painted wooden walls, and brightly colored industrial shelving for his wheeled beauties. Everything he cherishes has found a place here.

Besides the bikes themselves, including the stunning red 1915 Indian TT Factory Racer heading the pack in the front, there are vintage racing uniforms, helmets, gloves, photographs, signs, and along the back wall a colorful collection of AMA (American Motorcycle Association) safety award banners. Oh, and of course, in the background he's playing the most amazing soundtrack of his favorite country tunes! "After all," he says, "We're in Nash, Baby!"

THE
BRICKLAYER'S
STORY

Mike Wolfe is the ultimate *American Picker*, but not just of the things he's dug, pulled, hammered, and even thawed out of the weathered barns, warehouses, sheds, attics, and crammed houses he's explored all across America, but of the stories they tell. Take the beaten-up, patched, and weathered denim jacket taped on the opposite page. It belonged to an unknown bricklayer who carried in his pockets the heavy bricks he was laying until they split open the seams and he patched them over and over again. Mike saw this jacket as a poignant story of a man who would not give up on the vestments that helped him do his job. In those patches was a kind of dignity and resourcefulness.

It's not just an old jacket, it's the story of a man who took pride in his work. Isn't that why we all collect? Isn't it about the stories we find or feel or imagine in those forgotten things we hunt down on some card table at a yard sale along the side of a road or on the stoop of a brownstone or in the bottom of a cardboard box at a flea market? Like Mike, I think so.

Above: Wolfe family cat Rainbow Shine's eyes are almost denim-colored.

It's been about twelve years since Mike and his wife, Jodi, climbed off their motorcycle in front of a bar in downtown Nashville and a passerby noticing their Iowa plates asked if they'd just driven from there. After a "Yes," and an "Egad!" they followed him into the bar, hung out, and ended up taking a ride to Leiper's Fork, to see "the most beautiful part of Nashville." Years later in 2010, after becoming regulars at the Nashville Flea Market and making lots of friends they made the area their home. Expecting their first child, they went to see a piece of property tucked up in the woods. Jodi remembers that as they approached, before even viewing the house, she said, "I want to live here." She saw the trees and the creek and could imagine "a child running through it." That child is their now six-year-old daughter, Charlie.

At the top of the pasture is a "falling apart" 1915 fishing cabin that Mike restored and moved there, three rusty steel-wheeled Alabama tractors carefully set on the land, and a thirty-three-foot-vintage windmill. Mike sees it as "a moment we created where we can reminisce and reflect." Evidence of that is seen in the family moment pictured above.

If you are a Mike Wolfe fan, like I am, and can't miss an episode of his *American Pickers* adventures that he created more than eight years ago on the History Channel—then get yourself to Antique Archaeology, his hub in Nashville! It's a mix of treasures Mike's picked on the shows, his own personal collections (the bucking bronco, at right was a gift to me), and lots of great souvenirs like the T-shirt I'm holding up on the bottom of the opposite page. Mike chose the name because he was always digging in the dirt looking for what he calls "rusty gold." *(See Junker's Guide for info.)*

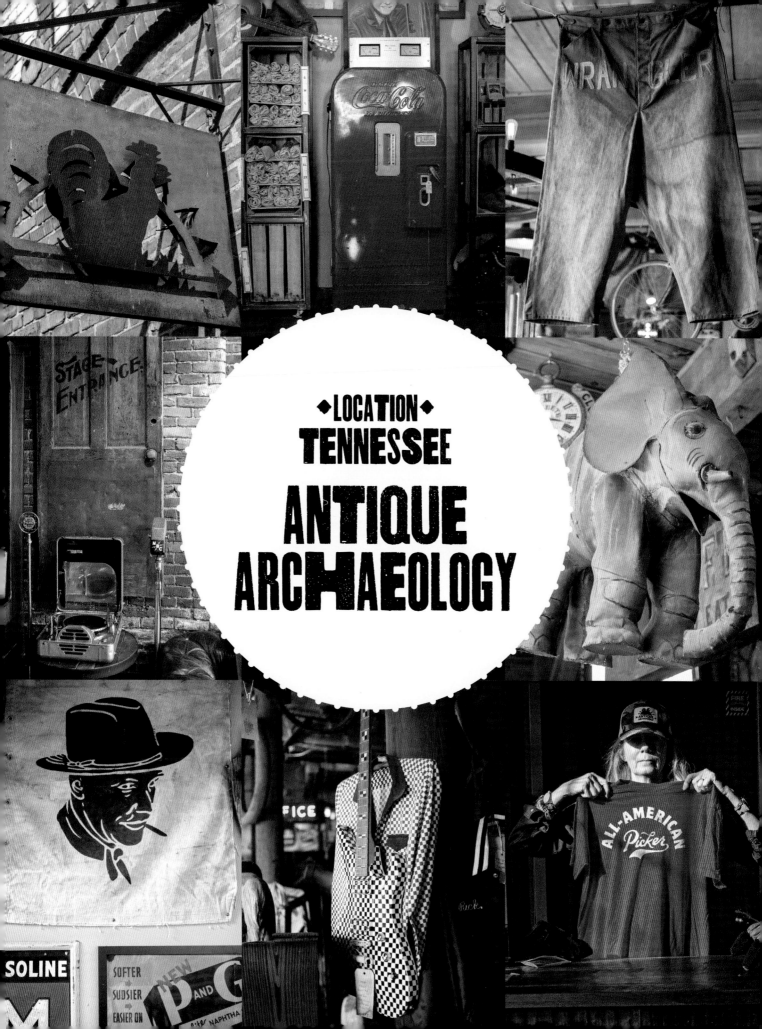

◆LOCATION◆
TENNESSEE

ANTIQUE ARCHAEOLOGY

SHARI ELF

LIFE IN THE SLOW LANE

Sometimes you have to give up life in the big city and retreat to a place where you can discover a little peace and quiet, which is what artist *Shari Elf* did when she traded Los Angeles for life in the desert, and lo and behold, found a place, not only for her creativity to bloom, but a home to share her now world famous crochet collection.

I'VE **STAR**TED BATTLING CLUTTER BECAUSE NOW I FIND BEAUTY IN EVE**R**YTHING.

SHARI

Shari Elf is the creator and curator (along with her crocheted alligator/alter ego, Bunny) of a very special one-of-a-kind museum housed in what looks like a giant lime Popsicle-colored camera. Which is exactly what the founders of the Photo Quick chain of overnight drive-through film processing kiosks had in mind. That was back in the 1970s, but the one Shari kept passing on the side of the road in 2006, not far from where she lives in Joshua Tree, was beige and long abandoned. She tracked down the owner who told her it was the last of its kind. Shari convinced her she would make it the first of its kind—the one and only World Famous Crochet Museum! The crochet collection began in 1998, with a pair of crocheted poodles her junking buddy and fellow artist Ramona Otto had pointed out at a flea market. At first she didn't see the beauty in them, but then, she recalls, after she started picking up crocheted creatures at every flea market and yard sale, "I'd see how great they looked together." What started as a little collection grouped on her bathroom shelves has grown to about one thousand pieces.

But back then Shari Elf (yes, that is her real name!) was living in Los Angeles making a reputation for herself creating art out of found objects. After moving to Joshua Tree in 2001 she and a friend decided to fix up some empty galleries in town and days before the grand opening of their Art Queen center, they decided it was the perfect home and time to launch the Crochet Museum. Shari got to work painting it, making the sign, building shelves, and moving her crochet family into what she thought might be a temporary home. But once the pieces were all happily squished together she saw very clearly that this was meant to be—a permanent home for her crochet collection, the now World Famous Crochet Museum.

Though not what the founder had in mind, twelve years later, the World Famous Crochet Museum is literally "world famous," having been featured in a national ad campaign posted in international airports everywhere. The headline read "It favours the unorthodox," which is what the many visitors to this unique outpost still discover as they step into the tiny space that's just big enough for an adult visitor to stretch out his or her arms in glee surrounded by the crazy, colorful, funny, beautifully weird handcrafted world of Shari Elf's curious crocheted community. No one has ever left without a smile on his or her face caught for sure in the snap of a selfie! Shari recently added a small unobtrusive can marked "donations" to the museum, which is open year-round with free admission. (Perhaps to support more crocheted acquisitions?) Who says a wacky crochet poodle can't change the world?

Previous page: The Crochet Museum in downtown Joshua Tree is home to more than one thousand crocheted pieces.

Opposite: Shari plays many roles dressed up in her handmade fashion finery at her Art Queen studio.

Above: A happy custom-crocheted tote for a tic-tac-toe lover.

Top left: The Crochet Museum is open year-round and is free to all visitors and selfie-takers, though donations are much appreciated.

Bottom left: Buddy and Bunny, Shari's crocheted sidekicks, take a breather on a granny square-crocheted blanket.

Bottom right: A fence exhibit of colorful crocheted blankets welcomes visitors to the museum.

Opposite: A scrabbled welcome hosted by a pack of crocheted poodles, like the first ones that inspired Shari's grand crochet passion.

Following pages: Inside the happy pandemonium of Shari's World Famous Crochet Museum. The latest guest (a gift from yours truly) is Little Miss Mouse dressed in yellow. Can you find her?

BRIGHTEN YOUR LIFE INSIDE AND OUT

In 1990, when Shari first bought her cabin, a 1960s Sears Roebuck kit home, a half-mile down a dusty road off Highway 62 in Morongo Valley, California, twenty minutes from downtown Joshua Tree, she saw it as "just a wonderful getaway." (At the time she was living in Los Angeles.) It was totally unfinished. There was no water or electricity. She lit candles at night and was perfectly happy. Then, in 2001, when she decided to move in for good she had her work cut out for her. After setting up a solar system to power things and a sustainable water system, she went to work applying her love of color to the outside and inside of her new home.

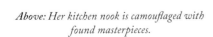

Above: Her kitchen nook is camouflaged with found masterpieces.

Top left: Blessed Mother watches over Elf-decorated boots blooming with succulents.

Previous pages: Shari's colorful desert retreat—a 1960s Sears kit home.

ARTFUL CAMOUFLAGE

The inside of Shari's sun-filled one-room cabin exudes a kind of upbeat fun expressed in the patchwork of turquoise, pink, and yellow hues she's applied to the walls, and the art that fills every special corner. She's wallpapered her kitchen nook, seen opposite, top-to-bottom with a collection of thrift shop paintings. In the living room the main attraction is an exuberant exhibition of cat masterpieces discovered in an old barn on a visit to Oregon. They are all portraits of pets owned by the proprietress. Shari bought four of them, and when she got home kicked herself for not buying them all. A year later she did! Whether you love dogs or cats it's a great theme for creating a collection.

Above: Shari's turquoise woodstove may have inspired the color of her wall. Bunny and Buddy, her two crochet mascots, rest on the bed.

Left: Sometimes people rent Shari's cabin just to have a visit with her cat collection.

When Shari found her 1974 thirty-foot Airstream trailer in 2009, it needed, as she puts it, "a lot of TLC." At first she used it as an annex for her collections, but when she decided to share it with adventurous travelers she started to de-clutter and beautify the interiors with special flea market finds as well as her own creations. To create an alternative space for sunning, and for sleeping under the stars, she surrounded a patchwork-covered bed with hearty desert succulents, galvanized drums, and seating for all. You, too, can experience Shari's way of "living in the slow lane," by furnishing your own outdoor space or simply booking a "glamping getaway," on Airbnb—Morongo Valley, California.

Did you know?

The first Airstream trailer was concocted by an American named Wally Byam in 1929. His wish was to build a travel trailer that would move like "a stream of air." Today many of his original timeless designs from the '30s are still on the road.

Opposite: Shari's airstream, seventy-five feet away from her cabin, has one bed inside and one outside for sleeping under the stars.

It's hard to believe, but Shari Elf was a late bloomer to collecting. She points to twenty-eight as the age she really got into the hunt, picking through thrift shops to find materials for her art. An old metal vent would become a canvas for one of her paintings. Then she started constructing art-with-a-message out of the things themselves. Take, for example, the green chair in the bottom row, outside her Art Queen studio in downtown Joshua Tree, inviting guests to "Wait here. Your soul wants to catch up." Reflecting on her life post-collecting, she admits to a slight "hoarding mentality" and a "clutter" challenge. "Since I started making art with more stuff I've started battling clutter because now I find beauty in everything." Conflicting with her appetite for rescuing the "cool stuff" she encounters daily at desert swap meets, yard sales, and thrift shops is her Virgo rising sign that is constantly imposing on her a need for order. "I have to fight that part of me that wants to rescue everything. I've got to make peace with that part of me that wants to keep things organized." Looking inside her Airstream on the following pages, she seems to be finding a way.

BUNNY WILLIAMS AND JOHN ROSSELLI

SO HAPPY TOGETHER

Two iconic collectors—a legendary antiques dealer and trailblazing interior decorator—work together, hunt together, open a store together, and then live happily ever after together...with all their quirky stuff—nesting hens, botanicals, whippet things, garden objéts, and all manner of blue and white porcelain. Never boring!

BUY SOMETHING YOU LOVE AND YOU WILL HAVE IT FOREVER.

BUNNY

How do two very distinct icons in the world of antiques and interior design end up sharing their lives and collections together? She, Bunny Williams from Virginia, grew up in the country with one brother and lots of dogs and horses, and a nickname "Garbo" that her father gave her due to her keen sense of the dramatic. He, John Rosselli from New Jersey, the youngest of fourteen, grew up on a farm with a mother who constantly drove him to estate sales and a father who collected everything from a Pierce–Arrow automobile to a pair of giant Belgian horses. She with a passion for interior design came to New York City after college, got a job, and one day walked right into his antiques shop. "The windows," she reminisces, "were filled with blue and white china and there was a huge seven-foot-high bird cage with at least one hundred birds chirping all at once and ten Whippets flying around. The place was chaos and packed with everything." Including John, who like her had wanted to be in New York and after quitting school went to work for a quartet of wild Venetian brothers who imported Italian painted furniture, which after many zigzags, led to his opening the antiques shop that Bunny walked into. She, being young and slightly intimidated, didn't get to know him until years later when she was working for the prestigious Parish Hadley and became his client. As time went on they became good friends loving to shop together,

and twenty-eight years ago on a trip to the Chelsea Flower Show in London, they got the idea to start a special kind of garden shop. They named it Treillage and opened it in an old blacksmith shop on Manhattan's Upper East Side. After that they were together all the time and when they decided to tie the knot, she joked with him, saying, "We had the baby first and then we got married." They closed Treillage three years ago, and though they each have businesses of their own, their shared passions happen in Connecticut in a classic Federal-style house that Bunny bought more than thirty-five years ago. Since John moved in they've added a glamorous barn with an attached conservatory, a log-built Parthenon, a chicken coop, gardens, woodlands, and of course, as many dogs as possbile! At home she tends her gardens, he cooks, and they both go off to hunt. They agree on what they like: "Quirky things," she says. Like their shared Aptware collection spread throughout the house and barn, John's chickens, Bunny's botanicals and garden pots, John's whippets, and as many unusual chairs as possible. "Things too pure are," he pipes in, "boring!" They want things that have "a little personality." And why do they still do it? "It's in our blood," says Bunny "We're obsessed!"

Previous page: One of a pair of leaping bronze hares by the English sculptor Barry Flanagan, seen inside the barn, behind the sofa on the next page.

Opposite: Bunny and John with their rescued furry pals—Bebe and Annabelle—surrounded on this page by other things they love almost as much.

Above: A miniature convoy of spiffily dressed carved woodland creatures loiters above a tiny set of civilized seating.

Top left: Though Bunny and John raise real chickens, John's brood of nesting hens is a quieter lot.

Bottom left: John's love of blue and white porcelain reflected on this needlepoint chair.

Below: At one time John had as many as ten whippets, now he only has replicas of them.

Opposite: A pair of elegant portraits of John's best-in-show—whippets.

Previous pages: When John arrived in Bunny's life, they took the original eighteenth-century barn down to its timber frame and built it back from scratch. She calls it "Homage to John Rosselli" as it's filled with many of his collections and their combined eclectic taste.

IF YOU LIVE WITH SOMETHING FOR TOO LONG YOU DON'T SEE IT

A few years back Bunny and John added a 1980s A-frame to their country world. Bunny had always wanted a weekend work studio to create her designs and work on her books and once she stripped it down and turned what had been four bedrooms, a kitchen, and a living room into one big space, she got her dream studio. On the lower level is this cozy sitting nook where she's resurrected an old collection of needlework botanicals collected years ago. "I had them in the apartment in New York and I thought they looked so granny and I questioned, "Do I really love these anymore?" She did, and so she put them away until she decided they'd have a new look and life in this more modern space against white walls and a poured concrete floor.

The lesson: When one of your collections has been in the same place for too long, it can become invisible or just feel tired. That's when you need to find a new place for it. It's an exercise that Bunny and John feel is "energizing" both for you and the things you love.

A GOOD THING

When Bunny Williams shops she can walk into a room full of junk (which she loves to do!) and "if there are good things," she says she'll find them. That confidence comes from many years of "touching and feeling" things that began with her first job checking in shipments for a prestigious antiques importer. "You felt it, you picked it up, you touched it." It has led to an instinctive knack that she shares with John for what a good thing is. For her it means "a beautiful shape, well-made. It can be brand new, but it has to have a good finish and it has to have a design." John quickly adds, "and style, of course, has a lot to do with it." "And that emotional pull that draws you to it," continues Bunny. But she admits that sometimes when you look closely things are not as they seemed. Her advice—"Leave!"

Above: Branches of green tower over John's desk in an Aptware urn, a favorite collectible.

Top right: An example of an antique carved chair with lots of personality.

PERSONALITY

As Bunny says, "It may have great quality, but it has to have a little personality. You have to have the high and low. To me, that takes the edge off. Our house is very comfortable. The dogs are on the sofa. I don't want anyone to come here and think it's precious because that is not us!" In the end these ultimate taste-makers don't see themselves as serious collectors who need the pedigree or documentation of every piece they desire. They buy things they love and put them together. Bunny says, "I find it more exciting to find something in a junk shop than to walk into a Madison Avenue store where things cost billions. To me that isn't a challenge! I think John and I are competitive shoppers. We're testing our eye constantly. We love a hunt."

Left: A peek from the barn's big room out to the plant-filled conservatory.

Above: *A favorite—a huge urn found in London that cost too much, but they had to have it!*

Who would ever have thought of creating a rustic pool house that resembles a miniature version of the Parthenon lined with tree trunk columns and a pediment (missing the Greek gods) filled instead with pine cones. Why, Bunny Williams, of course! An English house with a porch made of logs and the prevalence of Greek Revival architecture in the neighborhood made her think a Greek Revival temple would be perfect! An architect friend helped her with proportions and pitch and a wonderful local carpenter accomplished the rest. The outdoor dining area, complete with a working fireplace, looks out on the simple beauty of the stone pool just steps away. "John really wanted the pool, but I insisted it had to be far removed from the house." After almost twenty years, it is as beautiful as ever, and she has no regrets.

Above: Above the primitive antlered deer resting on the mantel is a wooden Thai ceiling vent.

For the last few years as a contributing editor to *Country Living* magazine, I've been traveling around to their four Antique and Craft Fairs that take place four times a year in Nashville, Tennessee *(April)*, Rhinebeck, New York *(June)*, Columbus, Ohio *(June and Sept)*, and Atlanta, Georgia *(Oct)*. I love these events. They're located on fairgrounds and in historic villages and are chock-full of great dealers and crafters from all over. They really bring the magazine to life! Usually, I hunt the fair and then share my finds with a great audience under the main tent and then sign my books. Hope to see you there! *(For more information go to Countryliving.com)*

◆LOCATION◆
NEW YORK, OHIO, GEORGIA AND TENNESSEE

COUNTRY LIVING FAIRS

Nashville, Tennessee

If you've never been to Nashville, well, the fair is another reason to go! And not only that, but you can also plan a visit to Mike Wolfe's Antique Archaeology (see page 113), and why not throw in the Grand Ole Opry as well. Be advised that the fair takes place outside Nashville proper in Lebanon, about a forty-minute drive from downtown. Almost everything on the previous pages were finds from my hunt at the Nashville fair. Did I buy that big black-and-white cow? Nope, it weighed about three hundred pounds!

AFTER ALL
THESE YEARS
EVERY
FLEA MARKET
HUNT IS AS
EXCITING AS
THE FIRST ONE.
CARTER

Rhinebeck, New York

Because our country home is only forty-five minutes from Rhinebeck, I rarely miss this fair. It's also a favorite because at the end of the day I can pack up my car with all my treasures! If you live in New York City, you can be there in less than two hours by train. Since it's a three-day event you might consider making a weekend of it. There are fun places to stay and eat. I've noticed many of these fairs are an annual event attended by mothers and daughters, even grandmothers. They all share that junker's DNA!!!

146

Wicked chickens lay deviled eggs.

QUEEN

JUNK

Columbus, Ohio

Of all the fairs, Columbus is the most charming. It takes place in a historic village so dealers set up their wares in authentic little buildings. Because the show is in September there are mountains of pumpkins everywhere. (That's a gleeful me on the opposite page in my fave painted overalls). While I was hunting treasures, my husband Howard (he wouldn't miss a fair!) was hunting down sweatshirts in the Ohio State bookstore! One night we explored the German Village historic district in downtown Columbus filled with shops, and the Book Loft—thirty-two rooms of bargain books.

Atlanta, Georgia

This fair is set up through meandering woodland paths where I ran into Sisters on the Fly, a huge sisterhood of adventurous women who take to the road in all kinds of vintage trailers and Airstreams. (See one of my favorites above, left.) The Atlanta fair has become a fun destination for them and for all kinds of stylish junkers like Anita Shegog, seen above, decked out in her crazy cool country and western junker's look. (What a pair we were!) And speaking of style—check out a favorite find—my "Pie-Ala-Mode" painted on a vintage enamel tabletop!!!

America's Little Darling

147

JOHN ROSS AND DON CARNEY

MEN AT WORK

Think of how much time you spend at work in an office or cubicle or just in a wide open space. Or if you're really lucky like *Don Carney* and *John Ross* who run a cool little shop in a courtyard in Boston and create their art and wares in two studios, a stone's throw away, then like them, think how you could work alongside the collections that inspire what you do! Find a way!

John Ross grew up in California. His first collection was paper napkins saved from the diners he and his family would eat in on road trips. He saved them in his Memory Box. Don Carney grew up in Massachusetts. He had an old jewelry box that he put stickers on to spell out "Valuables," except he spelled it wrong. Inside were things like foreign coins, a sterling ring, a polished rock: "Anything," he remembers, "that a little kid would think was valuable." It was many years later that the two met in New York City and started collecting together at the 26th Street Flea Market. By then they had begun to collaborate on designing one-of-a-kind handmade hats (inspired by one that John's mom had crocheted for him as a boy), as well as scarves, little appliquéd handbags, and eventually jewelry. To embellish them they were constantly on the prowl for old buttons, ribbons, trim, and any bits and pieces of things that would make them special. Sometimes they'd find a raggedy little falling-apart bag that might inspire a whole collection. They opened their first store the week after September 11 in a tiny space on Eighth Avenue and Twelfth Street. Because they loved the idea of combining unexpected patterns and things, like a crazy quilt's polka dots and stripes with wools and cottons, they named their shop Patch. After four and a half years they decided to give up retail to relocate to Boston to focus on their design projects. When they moved out of their little studio apartment in New York to an old house in Cambridge, "all of our stuff fit in the corner of the living room," says John. "We had all these empty rooms but ten years later we had filled it up." Now that they have lost their lease, those collected things are in limbo while the two of them decide where they'll live next. Luckily, their two design studios, gallery, and retail shop (Patch NYC, of course!), clustered together in an off-the-beaten-track courtyard, provide a home to lots of other inspiring collections. "We collect because we love the search, which always has the potential to be really great," says John. "There's nothing like finding a treasure and getting it home and adding it your other things and seeing how it fits in and even changes things." "The truth is," adds Don, "we love to make things, but mainly we just love to be surrounded by our stuff."

Previous page: One way to stay organized when you're constantly picking up small beads, appliqués, bits of jewelry—all kinds of decorative flotsam and jetsam to be inspired by—is to find a metal cabinet of little drawers like this one in the Patch NYC design studio. Each drawer is strung with the beads stored inside. On top is a paper collage by John and an eclectic display of vintage pieces that they can't live without.

Opposite: John's inspiration wall is filled with lots of paper.
Maybe that goes back to the paper napkins he collected as a child.
There are vintage photos, postcards, a colorfully stamped craft
paper package hand-addressed to them, wooden dolls and beads,
swatches, a pom-pom, and one of the first appliquéd bags they
designed decorated with three fabric leaves.

KEEP YOUR COLLECTIONS IN SIGHT

Things that we collect can become invisible if we store them away. Take a lesson from Don and John—leave your stuff out in the open where it can be seen and serve as inspiration. As John says, "It's just nice to have it out to see it. If it's in a box, it's lost!"

Don and John's design studio with an attached gallery where they host exhibits is around the corner from their retail shop, Patch NYC. One of its features is a row of open shelves filled with an eclectic assortment of collections assembled from their years of foraging. Though each of them is drawn to different things—Don's taste is to more fashion-oriented things, and John loves metal—the mix is what they love. A self-taught photographer, John also uses the collections as props for styling his photos.

Above: In the Patch NYC design studio, shelves of collections accumulated by Don and John inspire their ideas for photography, jewelry, accessories, and artwork.

Top right: To celebrate the release of their first Patch NYC coloring book, John and Don hosted an exhibition in their gallery of blown-up illustrations to be colored by their guests—like the owl seen above.

FIND/MAKE SOMETHING WHIMSICAL TO DISPLAY YOUR COLLECTIONS ON

When Don and John started their business with wool beanies hand-crocheted by John's mom, they used vintage mannequin heads to display their collection. Though they had plenty of women's heads, all found at a flea market in New York City, what they couldn't find were men's heads. So Don decided to make one himself. The dapper gent, seen at right, is his imaginative papier-mâché creation! Adorned here in their Boston art studio with masses of Patch NYC pieces, vintage inspiration, and other random finds, the mannequin is topped off with a vintage top hat brightened up with some kind of green flowered band. King Kong, to his left, seems puzzled at best!

Above: The dapper gent in top hat, Don's papier-mâché creation, shows off throngs of Patch NYC jewelry designs mingled with flea market gems.

Left: John Ross (standing) and Don Carney take a break with their nine-year-old rescue dog, Edith.

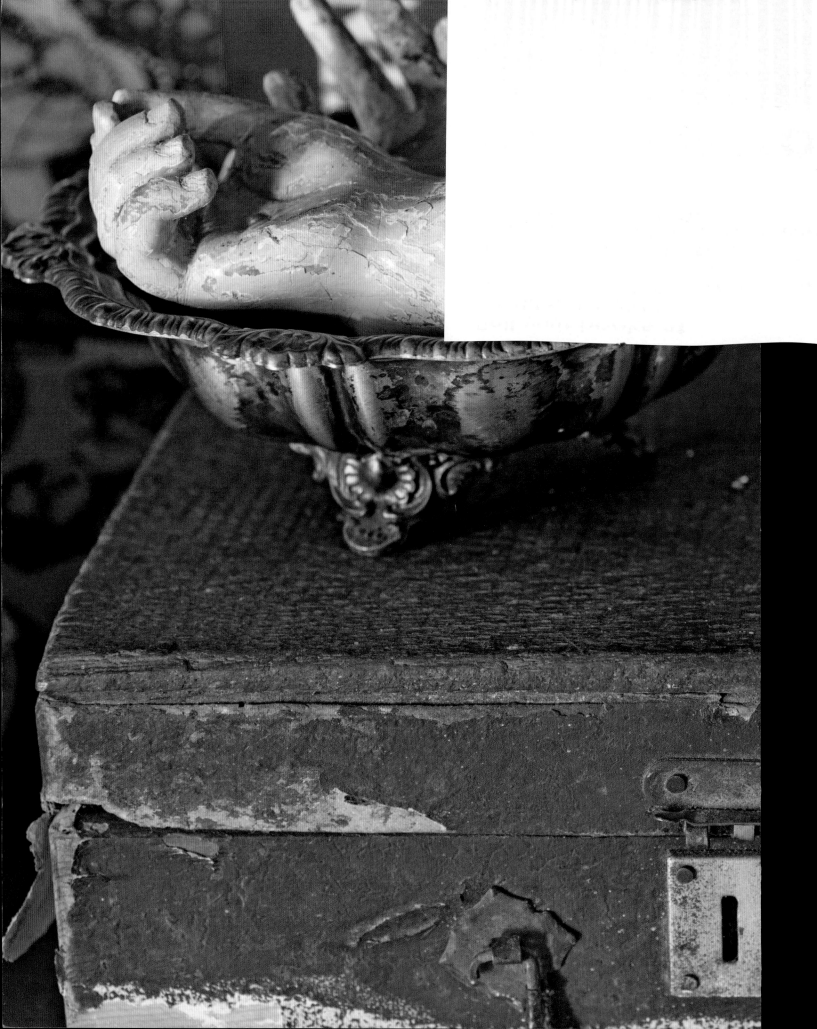

Once you're hooked on the hunt for things—call it stuff, treasure, antiques, or junk—whether it starts when you're young like nine-year-old Mary Stufano, my youngest collector in the book, or Corrine Warner who's not slowing down at eighty-seven, it stays with you like that indelible mark of a baptism. John got the urge when he was a kid going on road trips with his family. Don squirreled away his found treasures in an old jewelry box. They've never stopped! All the things, opposite, that they've collected—from the angel head top row, far left, to the vintage portraits of two very different women, second row, far left, or the fabric meats created by our friend Nathalie Letè, bottom row far right, or the old frames surrounding Don's woodblock-inspired drawings, second row, far right—live together in their studios, shop, and, most of all, their memories. Their hunt continues just like ours!

Previous pages: Among their shared collections are a quartet of expressive carved hands collected by John from vintage saint sculptures. Both agree these are especially nice because of the variety of poses.

Opposite: Collections laid on shelves, pinned on boards, tucked, and perched here and there in their studios and shop are only for inspiration, not for sale.

Above: This crazy quilt panel is from a piece Don and John hunted down in Massachusetts. Falling apart, a few pieces are preserved in a vintage frame. They think it looks like an amazing abstract painting. To boot, Victorian crazy quilts like this inspired the name Patch NYC. For them, like the quilts, it's all about combining different materials to create something new.

Above: This leaping deer probably once gave twenty-five cent rides to children outside a grocery store. Don picked her up back and she's been one of their mascots ever since. She lives in their art studio among all kinds of curious things, like the mysterious mask and lip pins behind her, designed by Don for Miriam Haskell, and other quirky, fun works in progress.

WE LOVE TO BE SURROUNDED BY OUR STUFF
DON CARNEY

Refresh your stuff: Don and John are constantly refreshing their collections not only by adding new things, but also by rearranging things. This wonderful cardboard mantelpiece (likely a prop for a stage set) is chockablock with a seriously curated display of disparate objects. It's a great lesson in the art of arrangement and Don takes credit, giving us a little tour and provenance of what will more than likely be a temporary exhibit. ("It changes all the time," he reports.)

Starting on the left is a glass globe covering a clay sculpture by Steve Murphy. It looks like an artichoke with legs and there are two more on the other end. Behind it is a trio of Don's block print—style art. When he became frustrated with his efforts to create real woodblock prints, he decided to create the look with pen and ink. Mostly he reimagines woodland animals like the very alert hooty owl seen through the globe. In the other is a flurry of feathers and next to it a beautiful vintage sewing machine. The two Asian masks, gifts from friends and collaborators from Paris, were meant to be them (John in orange; Don in blue). The fuzzy owl was a gift for Don's birthday.

LISA EISNER

YOU ARE WHAT YOU LOVE

It's very hard to pin *Lisa Eisner* down. She's fallen hard for so many different things—photography, fashion, book publishing, and now jewelry design. One constant companion on her self-discovery road trip has been her passion for collecting. What, you ask? Join her joyride for junk and you'll find out!

One of the very few consistent identities you could assign to Lisa Eisner is that of collector. That impulse—possibly latent at age ten when she ditched her Converse sneakers for a rodeo queen's tiara in her hometown of Cheyenne, Wyoming—followed her to the flea markets of New York City where in the late 1970s she hunted down one-of-a-kind vintage pieces as a fashion editor for *Mademoiselle* and *Vogue*, and then in the 1980s to Los Angeles, not so far from that mecca of all things vintage, the legendary Rose Bowl Flea Market. She and husband Eric raised their two sons in a one-acre Garden of Eden surrounding a kind of cozy 1930s "hacienda" of a house in old Bel Air designed by the architect Cliff May. That was more than three decades ago and though a second floor has been added (room for lots more stuff) somehow there is a surprisingly minimal, even peaceful, feel to these sun-flooded interiors—until, of course, you head back to Lisa's pool table showroom, studio area, and her upstairs closets. "I sort of have it under control," she says. "I'm not going to die in an apartment with newspapers stacked up, but I definitely have too much stuff." And if you look closely there it is—a coffee table artfully piled with crystals ("Of course, crystals—I live in Los Angeles!), walls of eclectic photography (Helmut Newton to Garry Winogrand), a perfectly preserved owl from Deyrolle in Paris ("we have great horned owls in the garden"), a lineup of customized Shriner's fezzes (inspired by the one her Grandpa Norris wore), vintage guitars (Eric's only collection), and tucked into little and large sacred nooks inside-and-out—altars to Buddha. And let's not forget her closets of vintage clothing, including a collection of Sammy Davis Jr.'s monogrammed tuxedo shirts and thirty suits she got at auction when she first moved here. It was five years ago that her insatiable quest for another passion—vintage jewelry, especially the Native American turquoise she had grown up with in Wyoming—inspired her to create her own eponymous jewelry brand. Before that it was Greybull Press, her own publishing company, and photography, and lately a cocuratorship with her son Louis of an artsy pop-up shop for the Hammer Museum called Rat Bastards. All these occupations/preoccupations have led her down what she calls "rabbit holes." "I need to be inspired and when I find something—a book, an article, a thing at a flea market—then all of a sudden I love it and I have to know everything about it and that's when I go down the rabbit hole. I live for that!"

Previous pages: Inspired by her Wyoming roots, one of Lisa's rodeo shirts designed by the legendary Nudie of Nudie's Rodeo Tailors of Hollywood. One of his claims to fame was the $10,000 gold lamé suit Elvis wore.

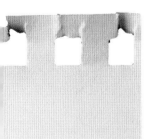

Opposite: In her home studio, Lisa's inspiration for jewelry (and life!) fills a thoughtful mood board and the space below it.

Following pages: On Lisa's desk a tooled message from her home state of Wyoming surrounded by her many passions— turquoise from her eponymous jewelry line, books published by her own Greybull Press and her ever-present Buddhas.

THERE'S ALWAYS A PLACE...

After she started her jewelry line, Lisa needed a place to show it. Not having a studio (yet!), she took over the pool room. She loves the way the natural light reflecting off the wine-colored walls casts a warm sheen on the bronze and turquoise elements of her one-of-a-kind pieces. To protect the table she's covered it with a thin piece of sheepskin. Surrounding this pool table feast are her collection of customized fezzes and a startling collection of more of the contemporary photography exhibited throughout the house.

Tip: Reinvent the Obsolete: If you own a pool table that's huge and immovable and never used, consider reinventing it like Lisa has or do as we have with ours in the country—cut a piece of plywood to cover and use as a spacious worktable or surface for organizing your treasures.

Above: The designer decked out in turquoise pieces from her own line, Lisa Eisner Jewelry.

Top right: Lisa's sacred collection of Buddhas lives in little altars tucked inside and outside her home.

Bottom right: The very tall golden standing Buddha with crystals at her feet greets guests at the entrance of the house.

Bottom left: A trio of miniature Buddhas mingles on a mantelpiece with preserved insects and Mexican crafts.

Opposite: Floating in a gold leaf niche, Lisa's delicate antique Buddha, offering the gesture of peace and protection, appears to live beneath the sea surrounded by lacy seaweed, corals, and exotic shells.

What looks like a galactic landscape from *Star Wars* laid out on Lisa's glass coffee table is in fact a creative display of her collection of crystals with two funny parrots on the lookout! Not long after she and Eric moved to Bel Air (make that more than thirty years ago) she met the legendary style icon Tina Chow who was an early believer in the power and beauty of crystals. That was it for Lisa. She started meeting gem dealers and collecting, and then made the leap into the big time by attending the famous Gem and Mineral Show in Tucson. "It's like the Rose Bowl of gemology," she says. One day, deciding her crystals were too spread out, she decided they should all come together. "So," she says, "I built this world on the coffee table." Does she feel that they give out any sort of spiritual energy? "I'm not so much into that," she says. "I really just love looking at them. But," she adds, "anything helps."

Tip: If you are interested in learning more about crystal collecting, there are gem and mineral shows all over the United States.
Visit www.rockandmineralshows.com.

DONT GIVE UP THE SHIP

CALIFORNIA RE

ART

IT'S A DAY FOR JUNK!

MOTEL ★GIFTS★

To understand this junker's ecstatic joy at finally arriving at the Rose Bowl Flea Market for the first time ever last July, go back to page 9 and take a look at the picture my son Carter Berg snapped of me just minutes after getting there! I had been anticipating this experience for far too long. And finally, I was here, ready to hunt the legendary flea of over 2,500 vendors who have been gathering on the perimeter of the iconic Rose Bowl in Pasadena on the second Sunday of the month for forty-five years. Take my word for it, it was well worth the wait! But wish I'd done it a lot sooner!

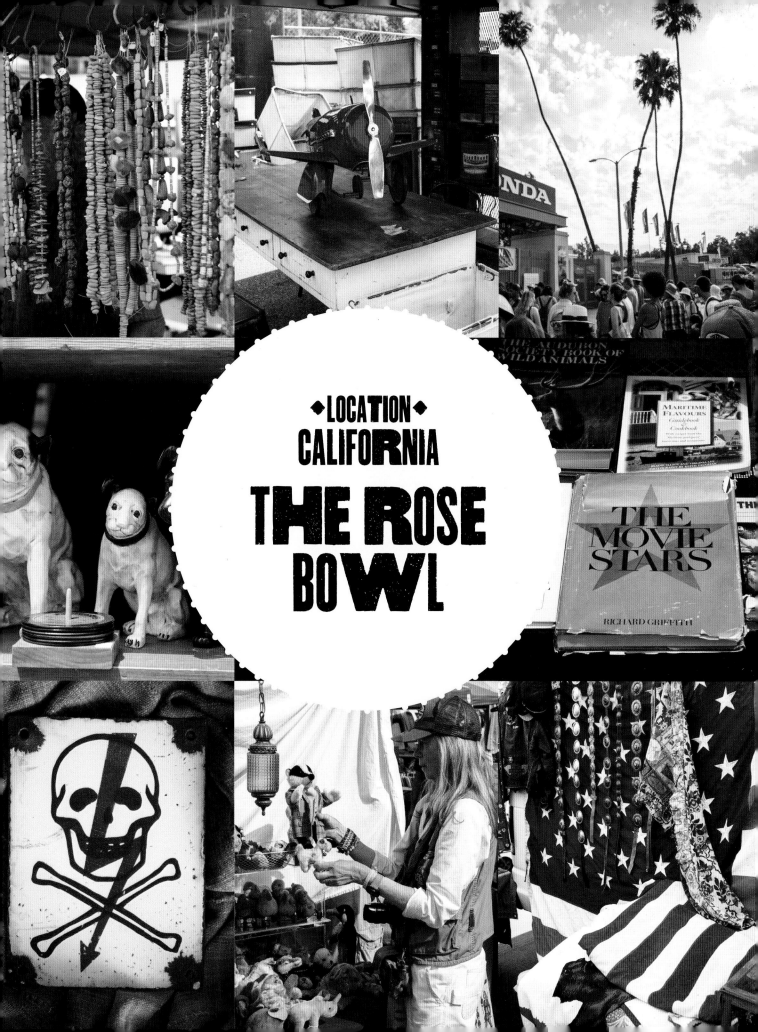

◆LOCATION◆
CALIFORNIA
THE ROSE
BOWL

Timing Is Everything

We arrived at the bowl around nine which is the time for general admission. Having been on these hunts for many a year my attitude about getting there at the crack of dawn is much more altered. I feel if it was destined to be, I'll find it! I was also helped by a list of dealers and their booths suggested by a veteran. This sets your path in a certain direction, but doesn't guarantee when you'll get there. (Yes, I bought the denim vest, seen below, covered with Scout and R&R patches!)

WE LOVE THE HUNT. IT'S A REALLY PRIMITIVE INSTINCT. *MARK*

Best Rose Bowl Find

What could be a better souvenir of my first visit to the Rose Bowl than a vintage sterling medallion shaped like the state of California? I pounced on it—from the booth of Mark and Lorraine Fogwell of Worn-Over-Time. You can find this indefatigable pair, seen at right, every second Sunday in the RB Orange section, Space P-1. Their specialty is very cool, very rare vintage jewelry and religious medals they've hunted down all over the world. My son Carter scored a rare skull and crossbones high voltage warning sign seen on the previous spread.

176

What's Free: Inspiration

Sometimes when I'm on a junker's jaunt that takes me to a place like the Rose Bowl where I can't easily throw my stuff in my pick-up and head home, well, you know—it's darn-right frustrating. So try not to focus your hunt on big things, but small things like the cool pieces of jewelry I picked up, or a vintage vest or jewelry you can wear on the flight back or a painting or textile you can layer in to your suitcase. But, besides all that, what is totally open to you is the amazing inspiration and collections of dealers like Mark and Lorraine and their friend John Dennis, seen below.)

You Never Know

When I walked into John Dennis's booth (right next to Worn-Over-Time) big vintage hats were not on my radar, until I saw the one John was wearing and the tantalizing one-of-a-kind collection he had artfully arranged on an old table. Boom! All of a sudden I had to have one of these hats. (See the one I fell for on the previous page!). Check out John's Instagram—samrobertsla and his shop in Ojai, California.

Rose Bowl Info

The Rose Bowl Flea Market has been going strong for forty-five years. It actually started off inside the stadium with dealers selling right on the grass. The merchandise areas are divided into five sections categorized by new and antique merchandise and by price. Go to Rgcshows.com to get a bird's-eye view of how things are set up.
When: The second Sunday of the month, from 8a.m. to 4:30p.m.
Where: 1001 Rose Bowl Drive, Pasadena, CA 91103
What: 2,500 dealers selling everything from vintage clothes, furniture, jewelry—you name it!

177

CORRINE
WARNER

MAKING ROOM FOR THE NEW

After living thirty years in a sprawling country house filled with large collections of folk art and outsider art, *Corrine Warner* at age eighty-seven decides it's time for a change, and after lots of soul searching, editing down, and a personal auction, she moves her old stuff into a new kind of environment—an industrial loft—and reimagines everything. What fun!

"Anything I love becomes a piece of art to me," says Corinne Warner as she looks around the new space she's recently moved into full of special things she chose to bring with her from four decades of collecting. The brick walls, concrete floors, exposed ducts, and tall industrial windows are the signature elements of an old cable mill in Williamstown, Massachusetts, converted into sixty no-nonsense apartments. It's a far cry from the four thousand-square-foot home in Dorset, Vermont, inspired by a horse barn, that she and her husband, Maurie, built thirty years ago. After he passed away she eventually decided, urged by their two adult daughters, that it was time to downsize. She had spotted an ad for the mill-converted-residence six years before and was drawn to the idea that it would present a very different environment and a new lens for how she viewed her collections.

But which collections? How to decide what goes and what stays when you've filled a house / a life with so many things, such as every kind of horse (rocking, weather vane, saddles, paintings), folk art, outsider art, and signs, just to name a few. She started with her favorite pieces, and then she chose things given or made by family members. In the end, she admits, "I had to let go of things I really loved, like the carousel horse, which was one of the first things I collected." (We were just married, she begins, "and had built a house with little furniture. I went out to find more things and instead came home with a carousel horse. When Maurie came home, he said, 'Couldn't you have at least bought an end table?') As well as so many other things that might not fit into her new way of life. So she held an auction. Friends advised her not to go to it, but she did. "It was very difficult, but it went well," she said. So she ended up with the pieces she loved the most and also demonstrated how she had grown in her collecting.

Three months in, she's joyous! "Perhaps it's the smaller space and the setting that excites me so and has helped me evolve toward a more contemporary and industrial look." She adds, "I guess that I just like trying new things. I like experimenting. Life could be so dull. Finding things that excite you makes your heart beat. Life's an adventure and when you're doing something you love you have fun." Corrine Warner's been having fun for eighty-seven years. She should know.

Previous page: Hanging above a bouquet of wooden kitchen utensils (and a bottle of marbles) displayed in a whimsical pottery piece with an almost invisible face is a painting of a tomato done on cardboard that Corrine had to have when she spotted it at a vegetable market in Dorset, Vermont. So, she bought her own piece of outsider art and the clip that holds it—for $40.

*Opposite: A table chair that had been a coffee table in
her former home now acts as the perfect throne for a wooden
carnival figure missing his nose and chin.*

HOW TO ADD FUN TO YOUR HOME— KEEP THINGS MOVING!

Before Corinne moved into her new home, she thought carefully about which pieces she would bring and how to use them in an unexpected way that would be surprising and fun. Look carefully and you will see a little snake, made by her daughter Laurie, crawling over the back of the striped sofa. And perched on top of the hefty armoire is a computer-designed rabbit made with a 3-D printer. It's like a game that keeps her collections moving around, so that often a visitor will say, "Did I see this last time?"

THE ART OF ARRANGING:

Corinne doesn't just plop things down. She looks for arrangements that send a message. Take the three strategically placed objects on her coffee table—a giant paper-mâché pipe, a triangular box that was supposedly used to carry a tricorner hat in the Revolutionary War, and a chunk of Lucite by an Italian designer. She sees them as a study of shapes.

THE BEAUTIFUL QUIRKINESS OF OUTSIDER ART:

Corinne's not sure when she first fell for outsider art, but she always has been drawn to its childlike simplicity and pure vision. One of her favorite artists is Jimmie Lee Sudduth, who collected pigments from clay, earth, rocks, and plants for use in his finger paintings—one fits perfectly between the windows in her living room.

GIVING COUNTRY A MODERN VIBE:

The industrial look of her new apartment instantly gives a more modern look to Corinne's collections. Take, for instance, how the wooden folk art horse now seems quite modern. Mixing in contemporary lighting gives another nudge to that transformation.

Above: Shopping bag art: An installation created by a French artist to mark the outlawing of plastic bags, he painted these with weird faces that inflate and deflate as they rise up and down. Spotted by daughter Laurie in a designer boutique in Los Angeles, this chorus line of quiet protesters now continues their demonstration in Corinne's library.

Opposite, top: Blooming Objects: "I'm not much of a flower person," admits Corinne, so instead she creates bouquets out of her things. On her coffee table she displays a tall glass vase of turquoise wooden shoehorns next to a squatty square one holding stalks of old tools. Under a glass dome nearby she's exhibited a prized find—an elegant brass flashlight.

Opposite, bottom: Rug pastiche: Corinne has always collected varieties of rugs. Her latest thrill is layering different kinds—an Indian, Oriental, and braided— on top of each other, producing an eclectic pattern-on-pattern look.

Right: Think out of the box: have fun with your collections by creating surprising juxtapositions and displaying them in a different way. When Corinne ran out of books to fill the top shelves of her newly built bookshelves, she substituted her collection of vintage cigar boxes. (See them on the top shelf starting on the far left.)

Below: Corinne wearing her signature large glasses (she has twenty pairs) and a make-do necklace—a vintage shoehorn dangling from a long piece of cord she found as-is in an antique shop.

Above: Corinne chose to make the second bedroom into her sitting room library. She watches TV sitting in the almost invisible chair seen next to her old wooden stepladder— the kind of contradiction she loves.

Out of the Closet:

Another testament to Corinne's love of simple utility items, often overlooked, is her collection of old wooden coat hangers hanging on a hook in her bedroom. She has picked them up randomly over the years, particularly drawn to peculiar shapes and those advertising exotic locales from Cannes to Harlem.

Did You Know?

History suggests there was no need for coat hangers before the Middle Ages since people were simply stitched into their clothes and kept them on until they wore out! (Yikes!) It wasn't until the 1700s that people actually started changing clothes and hooking them on to peg racks. Though it is suggested that the very clever Thomas Jefferson came up with something resembling a coat hanger in his closet at Monticello, the wire coat hanger was invented by O. A. North in the 1860s.

One-of-a-Kinds: *In her new space, Corinne makes a point of celebrating one-of-a-kind objects.*

Clockwise from top left: 1. A wooden trencher with a wooden folk art snake slithering alongside it are the odd centerpieces of a long dining room table. 2. A housewarming present, Mickey Mouse has become Corinne's constant dining companion seated in the "ghost" chair at the head of the table. 3. The old man in the moon, a motorized papier-mâché marvel Corinne found many years back at the Santa Monica Flea Market, shines down from the top of her bedroom armoire. She thinks his new home has put an even bigger smile on his face!

Opposite: The little hallway leading to Corinne's bedroom, turn right, is her favorite view in the whole house. She proved that even a small corridor can pack a wallop with an eclectic display of unique collectibles. Leading the way to a large black-and-white movie still peculiarly framed by a slatted piece of shipping crate with a handmade cloud hovering above is another of her signature pileups of disparate rugs. The weathered green bench supports a framed collection of photo booth snaps and on top of it is another example of outsider art painted and folded on cardboard.

A MOVABLE FEAST:

Corinne's always got sweets to spare with a pair of fake cakes artistically and humorously rendered by artist Frank Jackson (she found his cake on wheels at the Browns in Williamstown, Massachusetts, about ten years ago) and Vermont artist Roy Egg, who presents his cake cut out on a pedestal. The real thing, lined-up behind them, is her wooden cutting board collection, another sign of her love of useful things. The little metal bug (found one year in the toe of her Christmas stocking) is part of her miniature menagerie that she moves from place to place to keep things surprising.

Did You Know?

Cave men probably pounded their meat on tree trunks, which in fact could be thought of as the first butcher blocks! After the circular saw was invented and wood could be cut into smaller sizes, not only was it used for preparing food, but for serving it as well. Called "trenchers," they were a primitive form of our first plates. After that, cutting boards in all shapes, widths, and sizes, and made out of all manner of wood, became an essential tool in the preparation of food. If you pick up one at a flea market make sure to give it a good scrubbing. Sprinkle on coarse salt and scour with a lemon half. Let the lemon/salt goo sit for five minutes, then rinse, dry well and rub on a thin coat of mineral oil. After that you need only give it a simple hand wash—no dishwashing, please!

BOBBY FURST

RUST IN PEACE

Collector and assemblage artist *Bobby Furst* found the end of his rainbow on the edge of the Mojave Desert, but instead of a pot of gold, he found a pot of rust. This is the patina he favors and promotes as his mostly metal discards bake and flake under the desert sun. In this wide-open wilderness he's found a home for his art, his music and his quest for a more peaceful and sustainable way of life.

If you're ever in Joshua Tree, California, turn onto Twenty-nine Palms Highway, and look for what appears to be a ragtag military compound at the top of hill. What you'll see, looming on the horizon, is a series of corrugated metal Quonset huts surrounded by a curious graveyard of rusty artifacts with a tattered American flag flying overhead. This is the home, art space, outdoor music hall, veterans' memorial and refuge of Bobby Furst—artist, patriot, musician, and collector. I first met Bobby when he was living in Los Angeles in a 1947 bungalow in Laurel Canyon. I wrote then, in *Big City Junk*, that his house seemed to be an assemblage of his own imagination filled with the booty of his countless garage sale safaris.

Twelve years ago Bobby picked up all that booty—four garages full and a packed studio in Hollywood—and moved it to a house in Joshua Tree right on the edge of the national park. A big bonus was the three-car garage, a place to house what needed to be protected. "Everything else," according to Bobby, "gets better with age just being outside."

When we met up again seventeen years later, the landscape for his collections had changed—everything is now out in the open (baking!) under the hot desert sun, including Bobby, who has acquired the look of a weathered rock and roll prophet dressed all in black with his graying curls peeking out from under a furry faux leopard hat. Coming here was not about retiring his passions, but about switching them into an even higher gear, expanding his exploration for the unusual finds that fuel his creations. Beyond the normal flea market sources, he's discovered auctions at military bases, digs through huge corporate recycling centers, and of course is the recipient of the blessed loot bestowed by visiting curiosity seekers. "They see this place and drive up, and ask me 'What the heck is this place?' And, I say, 'It's my art studio. Got a minute?'" And then they get that special tour.

It all finds a home in what has become more or less a living art exhibit, a Bobby Furst experience often accompanied by the live music of transient bands who discover him through word of mouth or by stumbling upon the strange beauty he has created in this desert equivalent of the Hollywood Bowl.

When he wakes up in the morning, Bobby's first three words are, "Get over it!" and the next three are, "Make it happen!" And that's what he's done. Out of the collections of four decades, insanely organized in his three self-built Quonset huts, Airstreams, and other makeshift domiciles, stored meticulously in recycled cupboards, shelves, drawers, even galvanized trash cans—he continues to create and venerate his personal vision of a life lived in harmony, in nature, and most of all in peace.

Previous page: What looks like the concrete face of a bearded ancient is actually a Styrofoam stage prop.

Opposite: A five-foot wooden Buddha sporting American flag sunglasses, with one hand on a missile and the other peacefully extended sends a mixed message of war and peace. One of a pair Bobby bought for $300 at a local flea.

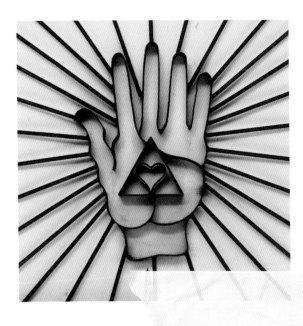

EVERYTHING
GETS BETTER
WITH AGE.
BOBBY

Top row, from left: A welded symbol of love rescued from an L.A. nightclub; a rusty jackrabbit that lights up at night; 1920s glass-front case lets you see your stuff; One of Bobby's anti-war oxymorons—bullets for peace.

Middle row, from left: Bobby and Carter share their common love of rusty patina; a ram skull sculpture; one of Bobby's Quonset hut studios built from a kit; an open-air fireplace on wheels.

Bottom row, from left: Perfect prayer for a collector's tombstone; the art of war—a 131-lined poem by a Vietnam vet spelled out in vintage wooden printer's blocks and bullet casings; a collection of ornate rusty crosses; a recycling system of galvanized trash cans.

Previous pages: A wooden peace sign stands like a reverential monument set in Bobby's desert world of rusty art and artifacts, Quonset huts and trailers, rocky hills and exploding Joshua trees.

MAKING NEW
LOOK OLD:
ADD A RUSTY
PATINA

All the objects seen at right exhibited in Bobby's rusty wonderland came by their patina naturally, but what if you actually wanted to rust something on purpose to give it an instantly aged look? Easy! Just grab gloves, protective eyewear, distilled white vinegar, hydrogen peroxide, and table salt. If your goal is to rust something small *1.* Place it in a plastic container with enough vinegar to cover, swish and *2.* after five minutes or so, pour vinegar out (If you're tackling something larger, you can spray the ingredients on out of a plastic sprayer.) *3.* Mix 2 oz. of vinegar with 5 oz. of hydrogen peroxide. Pour over or spray on object. *4.* Sprinkle salt all over and watch the rust start to show itself. *5.* Swish to rinse off salt and carefully pat dry with a paper towel. Go easy not to remove the patina. More rust will form as it dries. *6.* Spray with a clean sealer (like Rust-Oleum Crystal Clear Enamel Sealer) to prevent rust from staining other things.

A very good junking buddy of mine, Ramona Otto, had told me about this barn crammed to the rafters with antiques and stuff. It was located out in the middle of nowhere, an hour from Los Angeles in the Mojave Desert. I had to see it, had to hunt it, had to understand how a place like this could really exist. I felt in my heart that Antiques At The Barn In Lancaster, California, might be one of the last of a dying breed of junk emporiums being replaced by more sanitized shops and online hunting. I had a feeling it could just disappear into that hot desert air if I didn't see it myself! And, boy, did I!

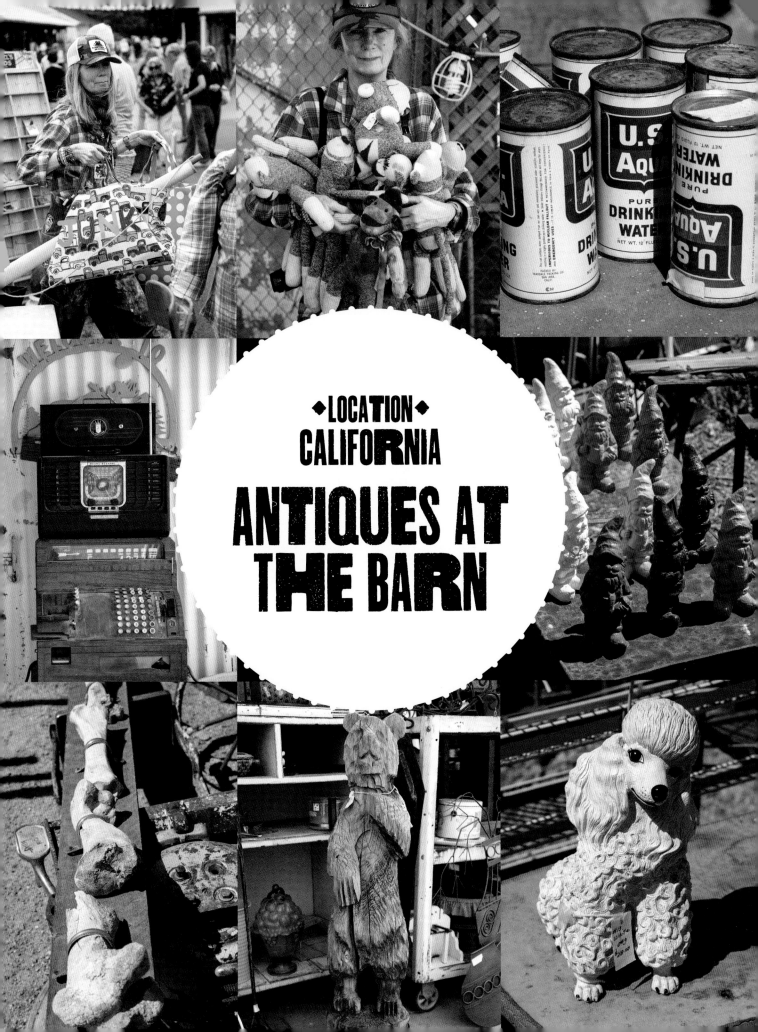

◆ LOCATION ◆
CALIFORNIA

ANTIQUES AT
THE BARN

This was my first experience with what can only be described as "Extreme Junking." That's because the barn is located in the Mojave Desert and it was July and 110 degrees. But, thanks to the Iowa-farm-girl-smarts still rooted in my friend Ramona, who kept handing me cold washcloths soaking in baggies and endless bottles of water, and her husband, Steve, who drove us there and kept the AC going in the car for cool-off visits now and then—we somehow survived!

MAKE SURE YOUR CAR IS CLEAN TO MAKE SPACE FOR ALL THE THINGS YOU DIDN'T INTEND TO BUY.
RAMONA

Ramona's Extreme Junking Tips

1. Hat, sunglasses, and comfy shoes.
2. Layered clothes that can be taken off or put on as the temperature changes.
3. Water.
4. Wet washrag in a baggy is very refreshing on your face when it's hot.
5. Sanitizer to freshen hands after handling items like Crispy Monkeys. Treasures at the flea are often very dusty or downright filthy.
6. Aspirin.
7. Snacks that are easy to eat on the go, like almonds.
8. A good rolling cart.

Joe Gilbert, seen below—bought the building and the site (an acre and a sixth) in 2004. He and Nancy had met a few years before, loved junking together, and thought one day they might open their own shop. Once they drove by the barn and saw it was for sale, they bought it over the phone, quit their jobs, and the rest is history. In the beginning no one came, so they advertised like crazy. "Now, we never advertise," Nancy says, "people just find us particularly during poppy season (the California State Poppy Reserve is just five miles away!) "It isn't an antique shop as much as it is a cool destination."

JUNKING IS AN ADDICTION. WE DON'T WANT TO GET BETTER!
NANCY

Inside and out I found treasures galore at really good prices. My favorite, seen on the previous page, was an armful of sock monkey dolls—an instant collection for less than $10, an amazing set of Elvis vinyls, an army of colorful elves (couldn't resist!), a six-foot wooden carved bear (couldn't get it home!), a giant Santa, hubcaps, radios, paintings (snatched a couple of those to mash in my suitcase), and a whole blessed section of sacred junk. This is a dying-breed kind of place—junker's paradise! Can't wait to return!

DANIELA KAMILIOTIS

A PASSION FOR FASHION

Growing up in Romania, creating costumes and set designs for the theater, *Daniela Kamiliotis* fell in love with jewelry. Whenever she went out she wore lots of it. Over time it became not only an essential part of her look and style, but the unique embellishment of her home.

"Ride a cock horse to Banbury Cross, To see a fine lady upon a white horse; Rings on her fingers and bells on her toes, She shall have music wherever she goes." That old English nursery rhyme has provoked many theories concerning the identity of the "fine lady" with "rings on her fingers." I propose Daniela Kamiliotis—a very fine lady, artist, and fashion designer who has used rings on her fingers and all manner of jewelry to define her very special look. This love of jewelry began when she was a young costume and set designer in Romania. She found jewelry as an artistic way of adding character not only to the costumes she created, but to the different roles she plays through her clothes.

As she emphatically states, "I always liked embellishments, and always thought jewelry was more important than clothing."

Fast-forward to moving to Manhattan in 1986, and into an apartment with her new husband, Thanos—with all her stuff! First challenge was to figure out where to store the large and growing collection of necklaces, ornamental belts, bracelets, bangles, cuffs, pins, feathers, flowers and rings, rings, rings.

As time went by she realized that storing them away in plastic bins, while useful, was certainly not inspiring. Very often she would forget about some of her favorite pieces just because they were out of sight. The solution, she quickly decided, was to make them a visible part of her daily life. She curated a special exhibition in a corner of the bedroom. Dangling things went on a series of hooks, above them went her collection of hats, and bracelets were stacked on candlestick holders, and a collection of vintage hatstands on a nearby table. She even put her artfully repurposed antique dress forms in the mix, using them to showcase special neckwear and such, (See an example on the previous page and page 212.) Eventually, the collection couldn't be contained and flowed like fairy dust out of the bedroom into the entire apartment, adding special magic wherever it landed.

And then after thirty one years, Daniela and Thanos moved to a new apartment (still in New York City), but with fifteen-foot ceilings, which according to Daniela, "made it look like a gallery—perfect for all the paintings and collections." This was an opportunity to exhibit everything differently, making it feel new, including her jewelry. Instead of hanging it on the bedroom wall she hunted down a pair of vintage vitrines in France (seen on page 214) and placed one on each side of the bed. She sees them as "cases of embellishments" and the pieces "not as jewelry, but as objects—installations of art."

Previous pages: Daniela's artful display of jewelry in a corner of the bedroom.

Opposite *A tattered toy horse found at a flea market was transformed into a magical unicorn encrusted with Daniela's fabulous finds. His tail is a vintage epaulet!*

Following pages: The art of living in a city apartment expressed in the disheveled beauty of Daniela's art work and collections creatively displayed on walls, easels, on forms and floor.

From top left: A tower of ivory and Bakelite bracelets stacked on a slender water bottle rest on a hand-painted shell-topped table; portrait of a girl by Daniela on a vintage garment adorns an antique dress form framed with sea glass beads; a miniature palette of Daniela's one-of-a-kind handcrafted rings.

Above: *Our Lady of the Rings is ready for anything wearing her geometric-shaped rings designed by Elena Votsi. She started with two, but loves how a multitude turns her hands into living art.*

Bottom: *Daniela's rings served up like confectioner's gold in a nest of her handcrafted and painted ceramic bowls.*

I'D COME HOME LATE AND IT WAS JUST SO EASY TO HANG MY EARRINGS ON THE LAMPSHADE.
DANIELA

After thirty-one years in one home Daniela admits that once she and Thanos had moved into their new space everything they owned took on a fresh life and look. Once she had dismantled her wall of jewelry in her old bedroom (seen on page 201) she vowed to create a different way of displaying it. The solution was a pair of vintage vitrines she found in a Paris flea market. She eliminated some of the shelves and found a way to hang her necklaces spontaneously. "When I see them in these beautiful transparent closets I'm inspired by them all over again," she says. "But then, of course," she sighs, "not all my jewelry fits into the vitrines so I am still faced with finding other ways of keeping it out in the open." An opportunity to do just that happened one night, when she came home late and was "too lazy," she laughs, "to put her earrings away, so she thought she should attach a net to the lampshade next to her bed where she could put her earrings and make it easy to choose which to wear the next day." Plus, "it was just nice to see them!"

Opposite: Above the headboard, which Daniela found on the street and gilded, hangs her tapestry to bring the sky inside. Her mannequin wears one of the many costumes she collects, topped with a harlequin's hat, reminding her of her days in the theater. The papier-mâché gold form was inspired by her love of Klimt.

CLARE GRAHAM

CABINETS OF CURIOSITIES

Here's a man who's spent his life on the lookout for small units of the same thing in outlandish quantities, like a truckload of 5 million buttons, 15 million poptops, and 10,000 yardsticks to respond to and create objects from his imagination, enough to fill a 7,000-square foot cabinet of curiosities.

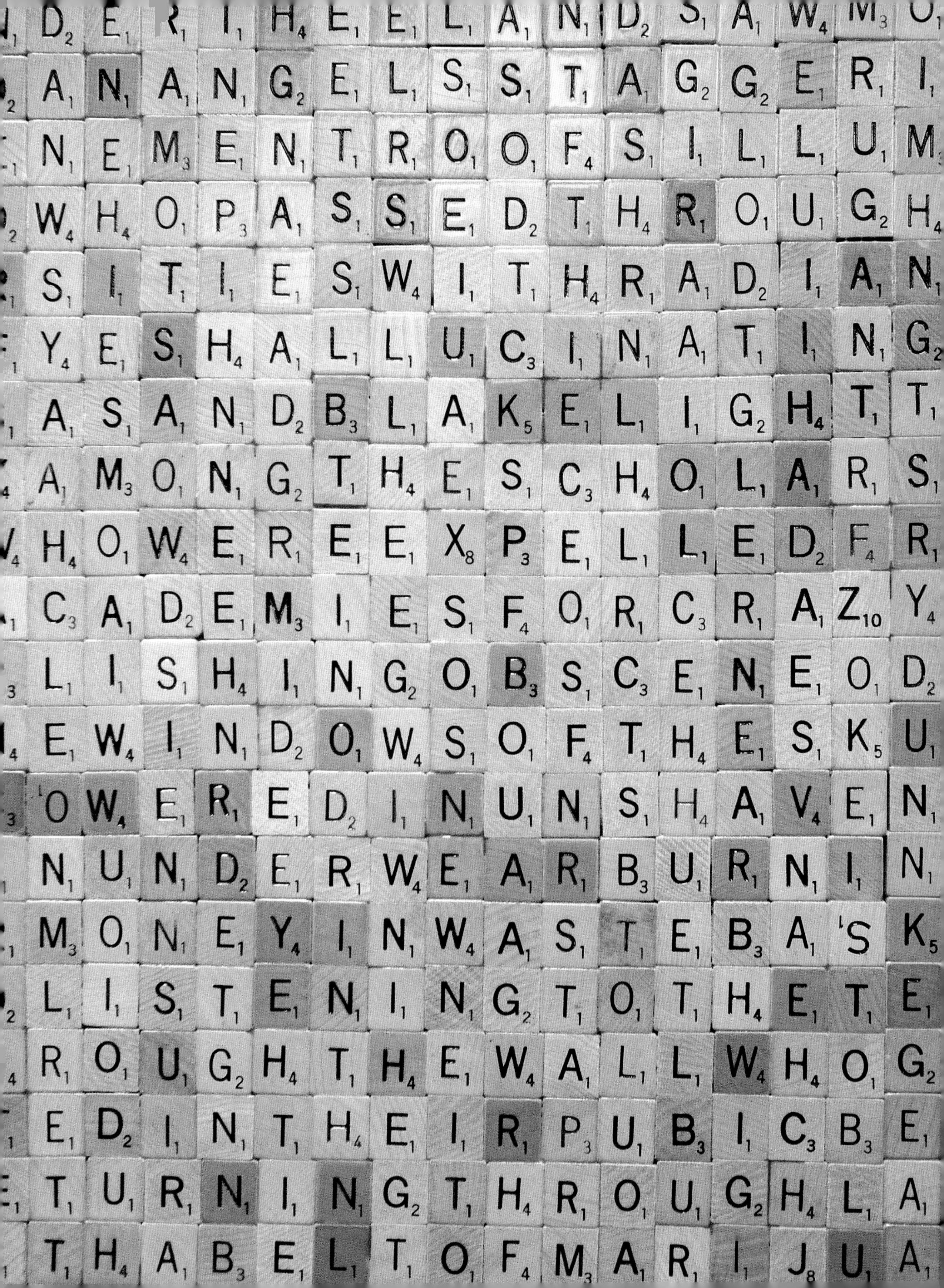

DERIHEELANDSAWMO

ANANGELSSTAGGERI

NEMENTROOFSILLUM

WHOPASSEDTHROUGH

SITIESWITHRADIAN

YESHALLUCINATING

ASANDBLAKELIGHTT

AMONGTHESCHOLARS

WHOWEREEXPELLEDFR

CADEMIESFORCRAZY

LISHINGOBSCENEOD

EWINDOWSOFTHESKU

OWEREDINUNSHAVEN

NUNDERWEARBURNIN

MONEYINWASTEBASK

LISTENINGTOTHETE

ROUGHTHEWALLWHOG

EDINTHEIRPUBICBE

TURNINGTHROUGHLA

THABELTOFMARIJUA

I have met the Wizard of Oz, and his name is not Oscar Zoroaster (Oz for short), but Clare Graham and he resides over, not the Emerald City, but "Moryork," a self-curated seven thousand-square-foot warehouse of wonders in Los Angeles. Originally it was a 1930s Safeway supermarket, then a roller-skating rink, then a few other things, before he and his partner Bob bought it in 1986. For fifteen years it was just a raw storage facility for his large collections of materials—a truckload of five million buttons from the Rose Bowl, leftover parts from the contents of a doll hospital, fifteen million pop-tops, five million titanium beads found in a salvage yard in 1968, 10,000 yardsticks, dominoes, bottle caps, jigsaw puzzles, Scrabble tiles, key fobs, rosary beads, owl pellets, chewed-up chewing gum, and an endless supply of teddy bears abandoned by the thousands at thrift shops everywhere. Looking back on his upbringing in the wilderness of rural Canada, the second of five children, he credits the gift of a rolltop desk at age eight from his grandparents as the model for Moryork. "They knew I needed a place to protect and organize my collections." (Of course he still has it! See it on page 225.)

And then in 2003, after retiring from a full load of producing big events at Disney he began to really focus on turning his materials into his special kind of reimagined art or as he prefers to call it—craft. "The trick is," he says, "if you get enough of any one thing it becomes a supply to assemble into other objects." Like the thirteen cabinets of curiosity he created for the Craft & Folk Art Museum (the inside of one, seen opposite, and more on page 223) with external treatments of dominoes, Scrabble tiles, paint-by-number forest scenes, etc., revealing on the inside a microcosm of disparate collections from used paint brushes to kachina dolls. Then there's the pyramids of yardsticks, the giant globes of twine, towers of rosary beads, pop-top furniture, and the wall-to-wall objects and floor-to-ceiling art pieces he's collected and curated together from local flea markets, antiques stores, and garage sales. He also relishes those things now relegated to what he calls "technical obsolescence," and points to a curious row of white porcelain cylinders that were once (before self-adhesive stamps) the central piece to an essential office supply tool for wetting the backs of stamps. He admits to having a magpie collecting sensibility but in the end finds all these collections and materials are fuel for his boundless imagination crafting artful creations out of the mundane, often obsolete, detritus of life, into his own magical kingdom filled with a storytelling mythology that would give even the great and terrible Oz a run for his money!!!

Previous page: From the exterior of the Scrabble Cabinet words by Allen Ginsberg, Chaucer, and the Book of Genesis.

Opposite: Inside one of the thirteen cabinets of curiosity is a tribute to the materials used in each.

Following pages: An eclectic cluster of flea market finds dangling from Moryork.

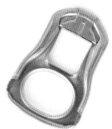

MORE IS MORE: RECYCLE FOR A CAUSE

Without raising an eyebrow, Clare Graham announces he's used about a million pop-tops over the years. Because they're smaller and lighter than buttons, for instance, you end up consuming a lot more while making objects. Clare sources them from metal recyclers who contribute sixty-five cents per pound to nonprofits like Ronald McDonald House and City of Good Hope. Clare offers ten cents more so everybody's happy. His pop-top chair, at left, probably gobbled up close to 80,000 of them. According to Clare, who tufts the entire surface with ten or twelve at a time, it's very comfortable as it distributes your weight evenly like a bed of nails!

Top right: A pop-top chair made of nearly 80,000 pop-tops.

Above: To win a Kewpie doll or cute stuffed animal, your sweetheart had to target one of these Knock-Downs, Punks, or Cats at the local carnival. Today, they're thought of as funky folk art and are hard to find.

COLLECT ONE THING

"The trick is," according to Clare, "to collect enough of one object that it becomes a supply to assemble into other objects. Take, for example, his domino cabinet. There are certain things like dominoes or jigsaw puzzles that are standard fare at every garage sale. You just have to stay focused and scoop them up time after time until you have enough to create something as unusual as a cabinet, a small entryway or coffee table covered in them!

THE ART OF THE MUNDANE

Old paintbrushes? I've always liked the artful look of one hanging on a nail, but Clare can't get enough and filled a whole cupboard, as seen below, with the "business end of brushes," as he puts it. He likes the patina of all these different bristles and fibers. When these things so ordinary are collected together they become extraordinary!

Above: One of Clare's thirteen cabinets of curiosities made extraordinary by a covering of ordinary dominoes.

Left: Inside the domino cabinet is a soft sculptural display of stacks of used paintbrushes.

EVERY ONE OF THESE OBJECTS IS A WAY OF KEEPING MEMORY ALIVE.
CLARE

Inspiring a Young Collector:

Being squeezed between an older sister and two younger ones and then a brother ten years later, Clare recalls being "very contained and private." Perhaps being sensitive to that, his grandparents gave him a huge roll-top desk when he was eight. He thinks it was in fact, a mini-version of what he has now in his 7,000-square-foot warehouse space. He describes what that desk meant then, "an endless environment for a child to organize and put things in."

Located in the back of Moryork, seen opposite, it's still one his fondest possessions. If your child shows an inclination to collecting, think of providing them with a place to display their treasures—if not a rolltop desk, then a few shelves or a little wooden chest or a set of boxes. It's an easy way to build not only their collections, but their confidence. You also might share the story of my youngest collector, Mary Stufano, age ten, who shares her collections on page 256.

225

Above: It took Clare about eighteen years to collect this tower of 3,200 rosary beads.

Top left: A cabinet of curiosities covered in little squares of paint-by-number forest scenes. Turn the page to see the amazing surprise inside.

Lower left: A pyramid made from a collection of yardsticks.

Bottom: Clare stringing his trove of five million titanium beads found in a salvage yard.

Opposite: From pioneer days housewives would save every piece of string or fabric and wind it into balls. These random globes of string and wire were found at flea markets.

Following page: Inside the paint-by-numbers cabinet, seen above, a rare collection of kachina dolls all created by one artist—Pedro Segundo, in 1972. Clare tracked them down at various LA antiques shops.

CROW MOTHER

MOMOLI KACHINA   KUNONA KACHINA   TURTLE KACHINA   STANDING CLOWN   AWATOVI SOYOK TAKA   KUTCA KACHINA

MOTSIN

23

KOHILA   HONGWA

JANE IVES

TALES FROM A DOLLS HOUSE

An actress who sees her urban loft as a stage set has filled it with props—doll parts, chipped cups, clocks-without-hands, and tiny bundles of cancelled stamps that connect to *Jane Ives*' life and create a mesmerizing backdrop for all the roles she plays.

Jane Ives was an actress for a long time, which is why, she explains, "my home is my stage set." And for the more than forty-two years that she's lived here as the wife of an artist (not for many years) and the mother of twin sons (now grown and on their own), today she is very much the leading lady of her own theater—a rambling loft of small rooms and cozy nooks propped out with objects that give dimension to the many roles she has played. They were hunted down in the places she has lived and traveled to—Maine, the flea markets of Brittany, Paris, India, and lately in upstate New York. "Each object," she says looking around, "carries a history of its own, but for some reason connects with something essential in me." She feels as if she is their "keeper," but just for a time until they pass on to the next person.

Over time, the personal connection is discovered. Take, for instance, her dolls. She states firmly that she was not a doll collector nor did she have many dolls as a child, but then suddenly eight years ago she found herself buying broken bits and pieces of dolls. Though as years went by it became less about dismembered parts and more about whole dolls. It was then that she realized the dolls were a projection of something broken in her that had started to heal. Her collections reflect not only who she is, but the way she has lived. "There are things that carry memory," she says. Like the little red stool that sits in her kitchen just as it sat in her mother's when she was a child. "I see that stool and I see my mother in her black and white bathrobe in 1951," she says. Then, there are the Flow Blue cups that line a shelf in her bedroom (seen on page 239). She started to collect them after her twins were born and her best friend painted a symbolic pair of them. "Most were chipped or missing handles, but that is how I could afford them," she laughs. After the cups came the Flow Blue plates, the clock faces, the pincushions, the wooden bird heads, the packets of canceled French stamps, Chinese checkers, croquet balls, books, and works of art everywhere. She looks around and worries about her "too muchness." "I had a boyfriend once who said I was like a walking lecture on 'dialectical materialism.' I think that meant that I was always in a dialogue with things." Maybe that's just another way of describing her love of all these things that prop her stage sets, that tell her story, that entertain all who enter her warm and magical theater.

Previous pages: Over time Jane's collection of vintage doll parts—heads, legs, arms and torsos—have been replaced by happier whole dolls reflecting, she thinks, her own life's journey from feeling emotionally torn to feeling happily whole again.

Opposite: The panting titled Domestic Patterns *hanging over a collection of Victorian pincushions, hints at pieces of Jane's collecting life--blue plates, shoes, the "watching" owls.*

Following pages: A personal installation of found things, mostly doll-related, arranged with great care by Jane to symbolically share her life's journey.

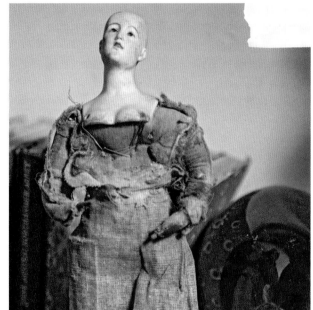

Top row: Jane's raggedy dolls; antique clock faces symbolizing "time is broken"; Dickensian twin dolls; the chips in this antique Flow Blue china are filled in with blue Magic Marker ink; curated odds and ends.

Middle row: Nineteenth century taxidermist's wooden bird heads; a happy book; vintage lead toy vehicles; a tortured doll heroine looks heavenward.

Bottom row: Colorful croquet balls; a chorus line of miniature porcelain bisque dolls; a vintage Solitaire game board with antique clay marbles; bundles of canceled French stamps; and Jane sipping tea from one of her Flow Blue cups.

IT'S NOT JUST THE MEMORY OF GETTING SOMETHING, BUT ALSO THE STORY THE OBJECT CARRIES. *JANE*

Curate a Giving Wall

Under the shelf of Flow Blue cups, Jane's first real curated collection is a wall of art created out of things given to her over the years. To add more dimension to her disparate collection of small and large paintings, watercolors, drawings, and decoupage, Jane hung a yellow wooden soda box on its side to display more romantic items—a pair of ballet slippers, a wooden racing boat, vintage books, and sentimental totems.

Tip: When curating a wall of your own, don't do as I do! Because I have no patience for measuring things and tend to do everything by eye, there are lots of nail holes under each piece of art that I've hung. If you're hanging a whole group of artworks at once, try different arrangements on the floor first, using masking tape or string to create the outline of your wall. Using picture hangers is a really smart idea, particularly for heavy pieces, and make sure you know the material you're nailing into—old concrete walls require different nails from plaster or wallboard.

Following pages: Ever the director, Jane sets a cast of diverse characters (miniature lead figurines) from the likes of Winston Churchill to a milkmaid and her cow, to a bugler, a drummer, Prussian soldiers, an Amish couple, and more on a floating stage shelf, creating a magical kind of choreography that is always changing.

NELSON MOLINA

TREASURES FROM THE TRASH

Since he was nine, *Nelson Molina* has had a knack for spotting what he calls "treasures" in the trash. Those special powers helped him detect and rescue more than 50,000 objects during his thirty-four years as a trash collector in New York City, leading him to create the one-and-only Trash Museum!

Nelson Molina started searching for discarded treasures—things people tossed into the trash—when he was nine years old. His territory was a three-block radius in East Harlem where he grew up. At Christmas-time, because he and his two sisters and two brothers didn't get that much, he'd go out and search for broken toys to repair and give as gifts. When it came time for him to go to work he landed a job as a garbage collector for the New York Department of Sanitation. Though he had applied for other city jobs, in retrospect working for the DSNY seemed perfectly suited to his hunting and gathering instincts. Nothing attests to this more than one of New York City's most improbable collections and best-kept secrets—nicknamed the "Trash Museum," it's located on the second floor of the Manhattan 11 Sanitation garage not far from where Nelson grew up.

It all began in 1983 when Nelson started rescuing small treasures out of the garbage bags on his route. In a short time his keen sensory antennae could pick out the difference between the clink of a soda bottle and the ping of a delicate perfume flask. The booty of those early excavations was stored in a 6 x 9' closet in the locker room. As the found objects grew in size and scope, Nelson categorized them and stored them in boxes, cages, in the basement, and on the roof. Fifteen years ago when a second floor parking area opened up, Nelson undertook the real installation of his collection. Setting up card tables, pool and ping-pong tables—whatever was available—he started pulling everything out and organizing it into carefully curated vignettes—superheroes here, a Christmas shop there, musical instruments here, and art exhibits everywhere. At first this paradise lost was shared only with DSNY insiders, but once word got out outsiders wanted in.

Three years ago Nelson retired, but don't think for a minute he has given up his reign over this special kingdom. Three times a week the "Mongo King," as he was dubbed, takes the fourteen-block trek from the neighborhood where he started this hunt to check out the newly rescued candidates dropped off by colleagues, including his son and daughter. If he sees something worthy he'll find a place for it. If not, then back to the trash heap!

The "Trash Museum," sad to say, is still not open to the public, except on a by-request basis. (See the Junker's Guide for more information.) But, not surprisingly, Nelson is happily optimistic that one day all he has saved will find a permanent home and be shared with all of us, who perhaps unthinkingly donated to this astonishing collection of trash-into-treasure!

Previous pages: He stopped counting, but curator Molina estimates there are more than 50,000 rescued items on display.

Opposite: Even superheroes need rescuing from time to time!
Thank you, trash crusader Nelson Molina!

Opening page: At the top of the stairs, the art-crammed hallway
that leads to the museum is a teaser of what lies ahead.

That's me and Nelson Molina—founder and curator of the Trash Museum, (bottom row, second from left,) taking a break from a private tour of the more than 50,000 objects he has organized into themes: from colored glassware to Star War *figures; from souvenir plates to campaign buttons; from the art of the city to portraits of disgraced heroes. At present the museum is not open to the public, but tours are given from time to time. Check out the Trash Museum in* The Junkers' Guide *for details.*

Save Your Memories

Old family photographs are probably the most precious things we own. They're the first thing we would grab if our home was on fire. That's why it makes a lot of sense to pull out those boxes and albums of dusty photos and save them from extinction by digitizing them. The best way to learn your options is to go online and search "how to digitize old photos." There are essentially three ways to do it: 1. Certain smartphone apps allow you to shoot the old photo with your phone camera and the app will do the rest. Only downside—it's one photo at a time. 2. Use a scanner and do it yourself. There are plenty to choose from at various price points and capabilities. Most scanners allow you to enter stacks at a time. Consider sharing the cost with a family member! 3. If all of this sounds like too much work, the third option is to outsource your pictures. You can send a box of 145 pictures or slides to Scanmyphotos.com for about 8 to 21 cents a scan, depending. No matter the method you choose—just do it!

Though there are things of real value in the Trash Museum, according to Robin Nagle, the anthropologist-in-residence at the NYDS, "The Molina Collection" is not a museum per se. (A museum is an official designation granted by the New York State Department of Education.) The good news is that support for an actual Museum of Sanitation, which would include some of Nelson's collection, is under way! (For news of that and more, check DSNY.com.) Whatever you want to call it, Nelson's "museum" or "collection" has given us all something to think about—"Should I throw this object away? Or is there a way to repair it or recycle it? Or donate it to a non-profit that will help others?" Thank you, Nelson!

Above: On a visit street artist James De La Vega left a message on this giant baby bottle.

Top right: In the sports memorabilia section, baseballs, cards, and bobbleheads abound.

WHAT'S IT ALL WORTH?

That's something Nelson has never truly explored because to him value is in the eye of the beholder! But sometimes there's more than what meets the eye. Inside the needlepoint pillow celebrating someone's pet golden retriever, Nelson and his sanitation sidekick discovered a wad of bills—$950! The bills, all from 1972, were so rolled up they had to iron them out. They took the money and bankrolled barbecues for all the workers. Other amazing finds: a memorial of 9/11 made from the steel of the World Trade Center (he tracked down the owner!), a signed photograph of Jackie Kennedy, a 1948 bike, souvenirs from New York's World's Fair, and the *Queen Mary,* family photo albums and diaries, signed books, pottery, Pez, pewter, records, Elvis, Mickey Mouse, even old movie reels that he projects in a little theater. Nelson spared no detail to give new life to these abandoned and resurrected things!

Above: Santa's holiday display stays up all year-round.

Left: Decorators would love to pick through Nelson's one-of-a-kind needlepoint pillow collection.

ALL OF THIS WAS FOUND BETWEEN 96TH TO 110TH STREET— IMAGINE WHAT ELSE IS OUT THERE!
NELSON

Sidewalk Free for All

Whether you live in the city or country, there are regularly scheduled trash pick-up days. That grand parade of stuff starts to fill the sidewalks or alleys or roadsides the day before, so be prepared! You've got to look beyond those fortresses of big black garbage bags for the good stuff that won't fit into them—odd pieces of furniture, lamps, toys, bikes, artwork—even musical instruments like those rescued by Nelson and on exhibit at the Trash Museum, seen at left. To be prepared, get out there early. I'll never forget the time I spotted a fab set of six hand-crafted window boxes a few blocks from our apartment. By the time I pounced on them, schlepped three back to the apartment, and returned for the others—they were gone! A better idea is to sidewalk pick with a friend—you haul; they guard! Or when you find something big, put out an SOS to a generous friend in the vicinity with a wagon or car. Trash picking is not for the faint of heart, but oh the rewards!

MARY STUFANO

THE BEST THINGS IN LIFE ARE FREE

When does the urge to collect begin? For *Mary Stufano*, age ten, it began, she thinks, when she was five or maybe six. Doesn't matter—she's hooked! Money was not an object. Everything she fell for was free! Here are some tips from a young expert on how to tag along.

WHY DO
I COLLECT?
IT MAKES ME
FEEL GOOD.
MARY

Mary Stufano started collecting when she was five or six. That was only just a few years ago since today she is ten. She started out with shells and rocks and sea glass, things she'd find on the beach with her family. Things that were nature's gifts because when you're financially dependent free is where it's at.

Later when her family moved to New York City, not far from the Metropolitan Museum of Art, Mary started her all-time favorite collection—the little round metal tags in sixteen different colors that indicate you've paid admission and which often become a kind of souvenir of your visit. The metal Met tags are a New York City icon like the subway token or an I Love New York T-shirt. Mary used to collect not only the tags from her visits, she would scour the area around the museum for others. And then they were gone! After forty-two years, in June 2013, the Met announced it would replace them with a more earth-friendly paper sticker. Mary, like many others, was shocked and went to the museum with her dad to find out what they could do to bring them back. "Start a petition," the museum suggested. "If you get more than 2,000 votes to bring them back, we might consider it." Mary was elated, but the task was daunting. And so her collection of these tiny totems became more collectible than ever! She has hundreds of them, and sometimes on a visit to the museum she sticks a bunch on to the front of her overalls as a kind of quiet protest.

Mary also collects beads. She finds them everywhere, in her apartment and on the streets. She's always got her eye out for more. There's also her toy collections—her little wooden train engines she's been collecting since she was two, her toy horses (she rides) and her dollhouse where Timmy her little stuffed turtle lives. There's her eyeglass collection, but she guesses that probably doesn't count since they're ones she has worn, but still she saves them. Mostly her collections are smallish things. Living in an apartment and sharing a room with her younger brother presents challenges of two kinds—space and privacy. But, still, she wouldn't give it up. She finds places to show off her things and places to hide them—"even in my jewelry case," she whispers. She's never been to a tag sale or a flea market. Well, maybe once or twice with her family, but she promises one day soon she'll go with me. Why does she collect? "It makes me feel good." And isn't that the very best reason of all?

Previous page: Mary Stufano and me, side by side in our decorated overalls in front of the Metropolitan Museum, New York City. Mary's bib is filled with the colorful metal admission tags she used to collect on museum visits. Mine are decorated with paint smears and a collection of vintage fabric patches.

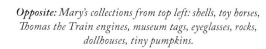

Opposite: Mary's collections from top left: shells, toy horses, Thomas the Train engines, museum tags, eyeglasses, rocks, dollhouses, tiny pumpkins.

Most kids are natural collectors. When my older son Carter was eight, he loved Canada Dry club soda and when he finished imbibing, he painstakingly removed all the labels and set these bright shiny things in rows on his dresser. But this inclination toward collecting didn't really show itself when he and his brother were younger and I would drag them along to a flea market. It was usually hot and they had not yet focused on a particular collection (like baseball cards, or Smurfs or *Star Wars* figures, which all came later) so they were totally bored.

Can't blame them. In retrospect, they needed to be prepped for the experience. Here are some thoughts:

1. Give them a choice. Come to the flea market with mom or stay home with dad and watch the Yankees (for example!). Or if dad's driving—stay in the car where's it cool and listen to the Yankees!

2. But, if you want to go hunting/junking with mom, here is five dollars (or less) to find some cool things and maybe start a little collection. Better they have their own money so they have to budget, rather than letting them ask you to buy them things.

3. Give them a little junker's bag to carry things in.

4. Watch your pace. Their legs are shorter.

5. Teach them how to haggle. A "can you do better?" from a child should definitely melt even the hardest-nosed dealer. (Oh, and don't have your children haggle for you. Not that you would ever consider something like that!)

6. Suggest something you think they might be interested in, but again it has to be their discovery, not yours. Just because you loved Mickey Mouse when you were little, doesn't mean they do!

7. When you get home let them share their finds with you.

8. Help them find a spot to display their collections.

9. If it's multiples like rocks, sea glass, shells, or beads offer some containers to store them in. Next time you can try to find them at the flea!

10. Have fun!!

Opposite: Mary standing proud in front of her carefully curated shelves of collections.

THE JUNKERS' GUIDE

At last, I know who I am—a ragpicker! In the opening essay in *The Keeper*, a hefty catalogue that accompanied an exhibit by the same name that took over the lobby and three floors of New York City's New Museum for far too short a time (July through September 2016), one of its curators Massimiliano Gioni writes of Charles Baudelaire's ragpicker as "the essence of the collector—not the kind that crowds auction rooms, but the collector as the ragpicker of memories and things: the *Lumpensammler*, the collector of the forgotten and of the disregarded, the lover of the inferior, who incarnates the drama and, perhaps, even the romance of an individual trying to complete himself through the objects with which he surrounds himself."

Without question, that's who I am. I love that reference embraced by Massimiliano Gioni and wear it proudly particularly on this Sunday morning as I wend my way through the haphazard trails of chock-full tables created by hundreds of antiques dealers set up in an abandoned parking lot squeezed between West 25th and 26th Streets off of Sixth Avenue. It is a universe of ragpick-ers communing for the weekend in an urban flea market to share and sell their curated treasures laid out on card tables or warped plywood sheets set on wobbly sawhorses under portable tents or strewn out on blankets covering the cracked asphalt like weird picnic fare pandering to the palpitating desire of browsers—tourists, city dwellers out to enjoy a sunny fall Sunday, or die-hard collectors (ragpick-ers!), like me, on the prowl for the unknown thing waiting somewhere in the piles of stuff that will quench our desire and fill our coffers with more old books, paintings, religious medals, toys—the flotsam and jetsam of other people's lives.

On the following pages of my *Junkers' Guide* enjoy the shared wisdom of the "ragpickers" that are celebrated in this book and wend your way through their favorite junking haunts (and mine!) across America! It is there you will experience the real Joy of Junk!

Junkfully,

Carter

Opposite: My friend artist Nathalie Lété captured a New York City flea market moment of me and some of my favorite finds. (Explore her whimsical creativity at Natalie-lété.com.)

CALIFORNIA

Antiques at the Barn
6851 W Avenue
Lancaster, CA 93536
661-726-9556
Open daily, 11 a.m.–6 p.m.

Art Queen
61855 Twentynine Palms Highway
Joshua Tree, CA 92252
750-660-5672
Shari Elf's studio gallery/gift shop is
always open

**Hi-Desert Medical Center Auxiliary
Thrift Shop**
6534 Park Boulevard
Joshua Tree, CA 92252
760-366-8660
Open daily, 10 a.m.–3 p.m., except Sun.

Holly's Trading Post
49700 Twentynine Palms Highway
Morongo Valley, CA 92256
760-832-5519
Open Fri.–Sun., 11 a.m.–5 p.m.

Long Beach Antique Market
4901 East Conant Street
Long Beach, CA 90808
Open third Sunday of the month,
6:30 a.m.–2 p.m.
longbeachantiquemarket.com

Pasadena City College Flea Market
1570 East Colorado Boulevard
Pasadena, CA 91106
625-585-7906
Open first Sunday of the month, 8 a.m.–3 p.m.
fleamarket@pasadena.edu

Pioneertown Crossing Antiques
55854 Twentynine Palms Highway
Yucca Valley, CA 92284
760-228-0603
Open daily, 9 a.m.–5 p.m.

Rose Bowl Flea Market
1001 Rose Bowl Drive
Pasadena, CA 91103
Open second Sunday of the month, 9 a.m.–3 p.m.

At the Rose Bowl:
Worn-over-Time
Mark and Lorraine Fogwell
Orange Section, Space P-1

**Santa Monica Airport Outdoor Antique
& Collectible Market**
3050 Airport Avenue
Santa Monica, CA 90405
323-933-2511
Open first and fourth Sundays of
the month, 8 a.m.–3 p.m.
santamonicaairportantiquemarket.com

NEVER ENOUGH JUNK!

SILK SCREEN — COTTON & LINEN
Custom
★ FLAGS ★
Tyler@CottonCalifornia.com
VINTAGE EFFECTS

worn-over-time.com

Sky Village Marketplace
7028 Theatre Road
Yucca Valley, CA 92284
760-365-2104
Open Sat., 6 a.m.–2 p.m., and
Sun., 7 a.m.–2 p.m.

Sun Alley Shops
61871 Twentynine Palms Highway
Joshua Tree, CA 92252
760-774-2553
Open Sat.–Sun., 10 a.m.–5 p.m.

The Mart Collective
1600 Lincoln Boulevard
Venice, CA 90291
310-450-5142
Open daily, 10 a.m.–6 p.m.
Themartcollective.com

The World Famous Crochet Museum
61855 Highway 62
Joshua Tree, CA 92252
Open daily, 9 a.m.–5 p.m.

Unity Home Thrift Store
61605 Twentynine Palms Highway
Joshua Tree, CA 92252
760-366-8550
Open daily, 10 a.m.–4 p.m., except Sun.

CONNECTICUT

Elephant's Trunk Country Flea Market
490 Danbury Road (Rte. 7/202)
New Milford, CT 06776
860-355-1448
Open Sun. from late March to
mid-Dec., 7 a.m.–3:30 p.m.

Michael Trapp Antiques
7 River Road
West Cornwall, CT 06796
860-672-6098
Open by appointment
michaeltrapp.com
info@michaeltrapp.com

FLORIDA

Renningers Vintage Antique Center
20651 US-441
Mount Dora, FL 32757
352-383-8393
Open Fri., 10 a.m.–4 p.m.; Sat. and
Sun., 9 a.m.–5 p.m.

4835 West Eau Gallie Boulevard
Melbourne, FL 32934
321-242-9124
Open Fri.–Sun., 9 a.m.–4 p.m.

GEORGIA

Country Living Fair Atlanta
Exit off of US-78
Stone Mountain Park
Atlanta, GA
Open annually one weekend in October
(check dates on countryliving.com/
country-living-fair/)

IOWA

Antique Archaeology
115 ½ Davenport Street
LeClaire, IA 52753
563-265-3939
Open Mon.–Sat., 10 a.m.–6 p.m.
Sun., 12–5 p.m.
pickster45@gmail.com

LOUISIANA

Antiques on Jackson
1028 Jackson Avenue
(corner of Magazine Street)
New Orleans, LA 70130
504-524-8201
Open Mon.–Sat., 10 a.m.–5 p.m.

To me, this little treasure of a shop captures
the true romance of NOLA. You enter through
Simon Hardeveld's outdoor studio of fantastic
art and junk installations into his wife Maria's
magical jumble of religious artifacts, piles
of Florentine boxes and trays, and weathered
books—tattered beauty everywhere.

Aux Belles Choses
3912 Magazine Street
New Orleans, LA 70115
504-891-1109
Open Mon.–Sat., 10 a.m.–5 p.m.

Dop Antiques
300 Jefferson Highway
New Orleans, LA 70121
504-373-5132
Open Mon.–Sat., 10 a.m.–5 p.m.

Southern Arch Architectural Salvage
3983 Tchoupitoulas Street
New Orleans, LA 70115
504-203-1391
Open Mon.–Fri., 9 a.m.–4 p.m.

MAINE

Big Chicken Barn Books & Antiques
1768 Bucksport Road
Ellsworth, ME 04605
207-667-7308
Open year-round, 10 a.m.–5 p.m.

Fort Andross Flea Market
14 Maine Street
Brunswick, ME 04011
207-442-0436
Open weekends

MASSACHUSETTS

Brimfield Antique Show & Flea Market
Exits 8 and 9 off the
Massachusetts Turnpike/Interstate 90
Brimfield, MA
Open three times a year: May, July, and Sept.
brimfieldshow.com

Hammertown
15 Bridge Street
Great Barrington, MA 02130
413-528-7766
Open Mon.–Sat. 10 a.m.–5 p.m.
Sun., 11 a.m.–4:30 p.m.

Patch NYC
The courtyard at 46 Waltham Street
(corner of Washington Street)
South End
Boston, MA 02118
617-426-0592
Open Tues.–Sat., 12–6 p.m.
patchnyc.com

MISSOURI

Missouri Plain Folk
501 Hunter Avenue
Sikeston, MO 63801
573-620-5500
missouriplainfolk.com
www.facebook.com/MissouriPlainFolk

NEW MEXICO

Winnow
28 Burro Alley
Santa Fe, NM 87501
505-795-7879
Open Tues.–Sat., 10 a.m.–5 p.m.

NEW YORK

Bunny Williams Design Showroom
306 East 61st Street
New York, NY 10065
212-207-4040
bunnywilliams.com

Carousel Antiques
611 Warren Street
Hudson, NY 12534
518-828-9127

Chelsea Flea Market
39 West 25th Street
New York, NY 10010
212-243-5343
Open Sat. and Sun., 6:30 a.m.–6 p.m.

Country Living Fair
Dutchess County Fairgrounds
6550 Spring Brooke Avenue
Rhinebeck, NY 12672
Open annually one weekend in June,
10 a.m.–5 p.m.

Fern
The Warehouse, 99 South 3rd Street
Hudson, NY 12534
518-876-2886
Open Sat. and Sun., 12–5 p.m.

Hammertown Rhinebeck
Montgomery Row
Rhinebeck, NY 12572
845-876-1450
Open Mon.–Sat., 10:30 a.m.–5:30 p.m.
Sun., 11 a.m.–5 p.m.

The Hudson Mercantile
202 Allen Street
Hudson, NY 12534
518-828-3432
Open daily, 11 a.m.–5 p.m., except Tues.

Hunter Bee
21 Main Street
Millerton, NY 12546
518-789-2127
Open Thurs.–Mon., 11 a.m.–6 p.m.

Jack's Outback
30 Main Street, Cambridge, NY 12816
518-692-8651
Open daily, 10 a.m.–5 p.m.

Madison-Bouckville Big Field
Antique Show
Route 20
Bouckville, NY 13310
Open mid-Aug., Fri.–Sun.
madison-bouckville.com

Mark & Larry Antiques
The Warehouse/Door 21
99 South 3rd Street
Hudson, NY 12534
518-363-5340
Open Thurs.–Sun., 11 a.m.–5 p.m.

McCartee's Barn & House
Fine Art & Antiques
23 East Broadway
Salem, NY 12865
518-854-3857
Open Tues.-Thurs. and Sat., 10 a.m.–5 p.m.
Fri. and Sun., 12–5 p.m.

THE QUEEN OF JUNK is?

Millerton Antiques Center
25 Main Street
Millerton, NY 12546
518-789-6004
Open daily, 10 a.m.–5 p.m., except Sun.,
11 a.m.–4:30 p.m.

Mystery Spot Antiques
72 Main Street
Phoenicia, NY 12464
845-688-7868
Open Sat., 11 a.m.–5 p.m.,
Sun., 11 a.m.–4 p.m.
info@mysteryspotantiques.com
My friend Laura Levine, the owner, is a
one-of-a-kind as is all of her wonderful junk!

Nellie's of Amagansett
230 Main Street
Amagansett, NY 11937
681-267-1000

Ole Carousel Antiques
Salt Point, NY
845-702-7622

Red Chair
606 Warren Street
Hudson, NY 12534
518-828-1158
Open daily, 11 a.m.–5 p.m.

John Rosselli Antiques & Decorating
306 East 61st Street
New York, NY 10065
212-750-0060
info@johnrosselli.com

Sage Street Antiques
114 Division Street
Sag Harbor, NY 11963
631-725-4036
Open Sat., 11 a.m.–5 p.m., Sun., 1–5 p.m.

Stephanie Lloyd at the Warehouse
99 South 3rd Street
Hudson, NY 12534
Open daily, 11 a.m.–5 p.m.

Trash Museum
New York, NY
Not open to the public; access on a
by-request basis
Call the Department of Sanitation of
New York Bureau of Public Affairs
646-885-5020

Warren Street Antiques
322 Warren Street
Hudson, NY 12534
518-671-6699
Open Fri.–Mon., 12–5 p.m.

HOMER & LANGLEY'S
MYSTERY SPOT
FOUND OBJECTS
VINTAGE
ICALIA
VINTAGE CLOTHING
ANTIQUES
USED RECORDS
PHOENICIA, NY

White Whale Limited
410 Warren Street
Hudson, NY 12534
518-755-6439
Open daily, 11 a.m.–5 p.m.

OHIO

Country Living Fair Columbus
Ohio Village
800 East 17th Avenue
Columbus, OH 43211
Shows in June and Sept.

PENNSYLVANIA

Renninger's Antique and Flea Market
740 Noble Street
Kutztown, PA 19530
Antiques, Sat., 8 a.m.–4 p.m.
Flea market, Sat., 7:30 a.m.–4 p.m.
renningers.net

TENNESSEE

Antique Archaeology
1300 Clinton Street, Suite 130
Marathon Village
Nashville, TN 37203
615-810-9906
Open Mon.–Sat., 10 a.m.–6 p.m.
Sun., 12–5 p.m.
antiquearchaeology.com

Country Living Fair Nashville
Wilson County Expo & Ag Center
945 East Baddour Parkway
Lebanon, TN 37807
Open annually one weekend in April

Serenite Maison
4941 Old Hillsboro Road
Leiper's Fork, TN 37221
Open Wed.–Sat., 10 a.m.–5 p.m.
Sun., 1–5 p.m.

TEXAS

Original Round Top Antiques Fair
475 Texas Highway 237
Carmine, TX 78932
512-237-4747
Spring and fall weeklong shows

VERMONT

Circa 50
4898 Main Street
Manchester, VT 05255
877-247-2250

VIRGINIA

Class and Trash at Scott's Addition
1720 Altamont Avenue
Richmond, VA 23230
804-716-5316
Open Mon.–Sat., 10 a.m.–5 p.m.
Sun., 12–5 p.m.

Sheppard Street Antiques
1126 N Boulevard
Richmond, VA 23230
804-355-7454
Open Tues.–Sat., 10 a.m.–5 p.m.

Verve
4903 West Leigh Street
Richmond, VA 23230
804-370-3765
Open Wed.–Thurs., 11 a.m.–6 p.m.
Fri.–Sat., 10 a.m.–5 p.m.
Sun., 12–4 p.m.

West End Antiques Mall
2004 Staples Mill Road
Richmond, VA 23230
804-359-1600
Open Mon.–Sat., 10 a.m.–6 p.m.
Sun., 12–6 p.m.

JUNK TO THE BEAT OF A DIFFERENT JUNKER —YOURS!

Most of the photos on these two pages were snapped in Nashville and Leiper's Fork, Tennessee. The beautiful woman in the blue plaid shirt at far left is Alexandra Cirimelli, the proprietor of Serenite Maison in Leiper's Fork. Puckett's Grocery is a great place to grab a bite, and don't miss some wonderful local music on open mic night. Oh, and that's me dressed in a vintage suit, shirt, hat, and bolo once worn by the street musician who used to play that one-man-band contraption Mike Wolfe gave to me right off the wall of Antique Archaeology! I had fallen for it on my first visit, and he said he would give it to me only if I dressed head to toe in the one-man-bander's outfit. As you can see, at left, I did!!!

Go to my website Carterjunk.com for even more JUNK. More favorite junking places, and where you might find me junking in your neighborhood!

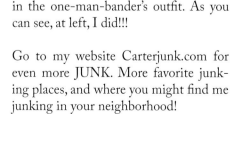

271

ACKNOWLEDGMENTS

A joyful thank-you to all the collectors who joined me in this book celebrating the things we have hunted down, stumbled upon, and been gifted that make us smile and be happy—Buffy Birrittella, Don Carney, John Dennis, Lisa Eisner, Shari Elf, Lorraine Wagner Fogwell and Mark Fogwell, Bobby Furst, Nancy and Joe Gilbert, Clare Graham, Jane Ives, Daniela Kamiliotis, Nelson Molina, John Ross, John Rosselli, Randy Siciliano, Mary Stufano, Corinne Warner, Reneé Parker-Werner, Janet West, Bunny Williams, and Mike Wolfe.

And all those that helped along this junkful journey—Meghan Aileen, Kasia Berg, Doug Bihlmaier, Christopher Branco, Sarah Buckholtz, Laurie Warmer Garrick, Lauren Grisham, Maria and Simon Hardeveld, Kerry Irvine, Thanos Kamiliotis, Stephanie Lloyd, Justine McEnerney, Roger Morales, Chief Keith Mellis, Scott Moras, Julie Nathanson, Ramona and Steve Otto, Neal Stufano, Gordon Werner, Charlie Wolfe, Jodi Wolfe, Mariano Testa and Rick Trabucco.

And with heartfelt gratitude to my son and photographer Carter Berg, my joyful partner in junk and this book—always by my side encouraging me, supporting me, and, with his creative eye and generous spirit, capturing the unique worlds of the collectors on our junk expedition across America.

A big thanks to my special pal the wonderful artist Nathalie Lété for her charming sketches of me and my junk on the cover and throughout the *Junkers' Guide*.

And to Aoife Wasser, my very good friend and the artistic crafter of all these pages. Her creative devotion to every image, title, word, and feeling has brought so much energy, real life, and character to the stories herein of those that seek a one-of-a-kind-joy-of-junk-way of life!

To big thanks to my Rizzoli team: To my editor, Ellen Nidy, who has once again brought such amazing insight and personal inspiration to yet another junkful volume. And to Charles Miers, my publisher and coconspirator on all things books for so many years and whose instincts are always uncannily right on! And Maria Pia Gramaglia for always making my junk look more beautiful than ever!

To Ralph Lauren, who wrote the foreword to my first book three decades ago, and then invited me to join his company. Thank you, Ralph, for always supporting my creativity, but most of all for letting be me!

And finally, my love and thanks to the man who has been my special life and joyful junking partner for almost fifty years—my husband, Howard Berg. And big hugs to our sons, Carter and Sam, who rarely protested during all those years and miles of junking journeys.

NO! THIS IS NOT THE END –
YOUR HUNT IS JUST BEGINNING!